KU-756-829

PHASE IV – 'WHAT DO I DO WHEN I'VE ARRIVED?'
Celebration time

I Can Do That! is dedicated to my Dad, Joe Hornby, who was made redundant in 1969, after 38 years as a miner.

It is also dedicated to you the reader. I hope that what you gain from this workbook will help you to quickly find rewarding and meaningful work – like my father did.

PASS IT ON

Do you have a jobsearch anecdcote which will be of benefit to others, or a novel way to tap into the unadvertised job market? 'Write to me at the address below. If we publish your contribution in the next edition, I will send you a complimentary copy of *I Can Do That!*

Malcolm Hornby c/o Pitman Professional Publishing
128 Long Acre, London WC2E 9AN UK

Acknowledgements

I am especially grateful to the 'Real Life' Career Planners and Jobsearchers who have 'test-driven' this book. Knowing how useful the activities have been to them was the inspiration to start the book, and has sustained me through many long hours at my desk.

I am also grateful to the people below, whose advice as critical readers has helped me in the development of *I Can Do That!*. Their candid advice (if at times difficult to take!), based on their experience, has been invaluable. I am sure that, in turn, it will help you in your jobsearch. Thank you. (Job titles at time of writing)

Gary Dickinson
Vice President, Human Resources, Bristol-Myers

John Lomax
Business Planning Manager, British Telecom

Roger Walker
Principal Consultant, Chamberlain Walker

Pat O'Brien
Principal Consultant, Patrick O'Brien & Associates

Christine Sanham
HRD Consultant, Christine Sanham

Carmel Capewell
CMC

Steve Dyke
Operations Manager, Courtaulds

Jan Denton
Manager, Opus, Devon & Cornwall Training & Enterprise Council

Jon Passmore
Chief Housing Officer
East Northamptonshire District Council

Robin Turner
National Sales Manager, Fisons Plc

Martin Scott
Programme Manager, G E Thorn

Nichola Balmer
Marketing Manager, Gent Ltd.

Jim O'Mahoney
Operations Director, Grand Metropolitan

Ann Keenan
Training & Development Manager, Hitchingbrook Health Care

Robert Appleyard
Production Controller, Ilmor Engineering

Ian Burch
Director, IRD Services

Soleveig Bruce-Stupples
Human Resources Manager, Pharmacia Ltd.

Elspeth May
Partner, KPMG Peat Marwick

Bob Dutton
Senior Assistant Education Officer/FE
Leicestershire County Council

Phil Laughton
Central Area Librarian, Leicestershire Libraries

Roland Powell
Manager, New Product Planning – Europe,
Lilly International Corporation

Sue Walder
Premises & Facilities Manager, NEC Electronics (UK) Ltd.

Margaret Gale-Smith
Corporate Training Manager, Northampton Borough Council

Linda Smith
MEC, The Open University

Brian O'Hara
Chairman, Penn Pax Products Limited

Tony Perryman
Personnel Director, Presto Stores Ltd.

Pauline Kinns
Training Manager, RTCC Ltd

Sadie Green
Freelance Trainer, Sadie Green

Tracy Smeathers
Personnel Officer, Scott Bader Ltd.

Rick Woodward
Management Development Manager, The Wellcome Foundation

Thanks to Sharon and Katie who turned my hieroglyphics into a neatly word-processed document, Richard who did the illustrations, Frank and John at Gemini who turned it all into a book and Pitman who brought *I Can Do That!* to you!

Equal Opportunity Statement: I have made every effort to make the text of this book non-discriminatory. If I have failed in any part, please let me know, so that I can correct it for future editions   M.H.

'Which way do I go from here?' asked Alice

'That'... replied the Cheshire Cat ...
'depends where you want to get to'

LEWIS CARROLL

Introduction

I can give you a six word formula for success: 'Think things through – then follow through.'

EDWARD RICKENBACKER

Welcome to *I Can Do That!* I hope you will enjoy participating in the activities, and that they will help you to take control of your life, plan your career and get the job you want.

For most of us, our working and personal lives are intertwined. Career planning is the process of formulating goals, for what we want to achieve in our working lives. This has an inevitable impact on our personal lives.

Without goals, your career (and your life) could be shaped by accident, fate or even by the decisions by other people. This may lead to dissatisfaction or frustration. By **setting your own goals**, you can take control of your own career development and your own life.

The foundation of our career and life planning process is knowing **who you are**. Being able to identify your own strengths, skills and values, is vital in setting realistic career goals. These will help you to make decisions about your career and about opportunities available to you.

By working through the activities in this book you will have a clearer idea of where you are now, where you are going and how you will get there.

Self-assessment

The first phase is 'Understanding Myself'. This will help you to develop a more enlightened picture of who you are and what you want out of life.

We will then go on to identify how you can match your skills to jobs effectively through a greater personal understanding and an understanding of how to secure a new job.

Not all the sections in this workbook will be equally relevant to you. Your own career and life situation, age, position, values, etc., will determine the areas you need to explore in greatest depth.

People change. Your interests and goals may change over time. By completing this workbook, you are embarking on a process, through which you will be able to establish realistic career goals and an action plan to achieve them: not just where you want to go, but also what you have to do to get there. You will learn to manage your career so that you can make informed judgements about the job opportunities that become available to you in the future.

Up, sideways, down

A 'promotion' is one way of developing in your career. However, it isn't the only way, and as organisations become 'leaner' and reduce the number of levels, the opportunities are becoming less.

Enriching your present position can be another important form of career development. So is acquiring a new set of skills, or taking on a temporary developmental assignment. In some cases, your best decision may be to move laterally into another area, or perhaps even take a step downwards to acquire new skills and experience.

You are responsible for your career and your life

The responsibility for managing your career is yours. **Take the initiative.**

Remember that **your career is only one important strand in the fabric of your life.** The decisions you make about your career can have an impact on other dimensions of your life – just as the decisions you make in your personal life can affect your career. The exercises in this workbook will help you develop a greater awareness of what you need to do to keep all the dimensions of your life in healthy balance.

Keep an open mind and be flexible

People often have problems in making career plans and developing goals because they impose barriers on themselves. They say to themselves things like 'I could never achieve this', 'That opportunity is not available to me', 'This isn't feasible' etc.

Keep an open mind as you work through the activities in this book. As a general rule people impose more restrictions on themselves, than are imposed on them by other people.

Invest in yourself

Don't be put off by the length of this workbook. It won't take long to complete.

Complete one or two exercises at a time. You will get the best benefit if you complete the workbook in a continuous period of two to four weeks. You will find the process takes on a momentum of its own.

The benefits you obtain from this workbook will be in direct proportion to the effort you put into completing them. It may be tempting to read through the exercises and 'complete them in your head'. Do that as a starting point, but you will only really benefit by sitting down, pencil in hand!

Concentrate on areas relevant to you

As already mentioned, not all sections of this workbook will be equally relevant to you.

Consult others

Career and life planning means integrating information about you – your interests, skills and potential. You will understand yourself better if you check your own perceptions against those of people who know you well – your friends, partner, colleagues, etc.

But before we begin, some ground rules.

- This workbook is about you.
- To get the best out of the exercise you need to be as open and honest with yourself as you can.
- At times I will suggest that you might want to discuss certain aspects confidentially with other people. This will give you the opportunity to 'test' some of your ideas. Remember, what you let other people know about you and what you decide to keep close is entirely in your control.
- You may wish to keep your workbook somewhere private
- We are all unique and for that reason each person will derive different benefits from different exercises. The common threads will be: **improved self-awareness and a greater chance of securing the right job for you.**
- It is not essential to complete every exercise.
- **There is a job out there for you.**

Good luck.

Malcolm Hornby

WHO AM I?

cutive/Acc...
..strator Advertising...
aftEngineerAirlinePilotA...
..malTechnicianAnthropologis
,oksellerAntiqueDealerArchaeo.
..rchitectArchiverArtDealerAstron
\uctioneerBalletDancerBankerBarr
BiochemistBotanistBooksellerBroaa
BrokerBuilderCareersAdvisorCart
CardiologistChemicalEngineerChii
ClerkCoastguardCommunityWorkei
,cretaryComputerEngineerConductt
'ignerDentistDevelopmentEngin~
'torDispensingOpticianDocto1
'ainerDraughtsmanDriving,
:istEconomistEditorEducat
calEngineerElectronicEngii
ainerEnvironmentalH~~1~
iomistEstateAgentE
,ortAgentFabricDesig
,rmManagerFashionPh
,ilmDirectorFinancialMa
,ishFarmerFlightControllerI
nologistFootwearManufacture.
OfficeExecutiveForensicScientist,
'orwarderGameKeeperGeneticistG

,rographicSurvey,
,ormationScientistInsura
,teriorDesignerInternational,
,velleryDesignerJournalistLand,
,wyerLegalAccountantLibrarian1
ousekeeperLossAdjusterMagazine
/lanagementAccountantMarineEng,
'larketingManagerMediaPlannerM,
,nysicistMerchantBankerMetallurgi,
,MicrobiologistMissionaryModelMu'
JavalArchitectNeurophysiologistN'
'ngineerNurseOccupationalThera'
ceManagerOpticianPackagin,
,terPatentAgentPersonnelM
'macistPhysicistPianistPoli
,terProbationOfficerPsychii
'~hlicAdministratorPublis,
reationalManagerR,
agerSchoolInspector,
,ersonSilversmithSocio
okerSurveyorSystemsA1,
TextileDesignerTheatreMa1,
,gStandardsOfficerTravelAgen
,erwriterVeterinarySurgeonWatei
,uthWorkerZooKeeperZoologistZ

Introduction to Phase I

All things I thought I knew; but now confess the more I know I know, I know the less.

JOHN OWEN

ARE YOU A FROG OR A PIKE?

Frogs are remarkably adaptable creatures. Apparently, if you expose them to near-freezing conditions they have the ability to slow down their metabolism and to go into hibernation. If you then take one of these frogs and place it in cold water, it becomes more active and increases its metabolism. As the water temperature increases, so does the activity of the frog. The frog makes no attempt to escape from its surroundings ... even if the temperature of the water is increased to the point where it is boiled to death!

So while being adaptable, the frog fails to challenge what is happening around it. By being unprepared to move to a different environment, the frog pays the price of its life.

In a similar sort of way, if you take a pike and place it in a large aquarium and then add a few minnows, I am sure you will not be surprised to hear that the minnows are very quickly eaten by the pike.

If a glass partition is now placed in the aquarium with the pike in one half and more minnows in the other half, the pike will make attempt after attempt to eat the minnows, but only succeeds in hitting the glass! The pike finally learns that attacking the minnows is an impossible task.

If the glass partition is now removed and the minnows and pike are allowed to swim freely in the tank you might 'naturally' imagine that the pike would resume eating. Surprisingly, the pike fails to recognise that the environment has changed and does not eat the minnows. In fact the pike will starve to death!

HOW CAN I DEVELOP A RECIPE FOR SUCCESS?

A major step may be to challenge your paradigm:

A paradigm is a set of rules and regulations that describe boundaries and tell you what to do to be successful within those boundaries.

(definition by Joel A. Barker, author of *Discovering the Future*, ILI Press)

But of course frogs and pikes are very simple animals. Human beings are far more sophisticated and should be more open to change ... would that it were the case! Most of us try to find solutions to our problems using our current paradigm of the situation. For example doctors use their medical training to form a diagnosis. This works well until either we cannot solve a problem using our paradigm, or someone generates another totally different paradigm for solving the problem which we will not accept. For example many doctors do not recognise 'fringe medicine' such as acupuncture because, in spite of any success, those approaches do not confirm to their own training and beliefs.

In business, people are blinded by their current paradigms to new approaches, whether they are developed internally or by competitors. Swiss watch manufacturers dismissed the concept of the Quartz watch, the prototype of which was created in 1967 by the Swiss Watch Federation. Before World War II the Swiss had 90 per cent of the watch market, by the 1970s they had 60 per cent but by 1980 they had only 22 per cent.

Similarly, 42 photographic companies rejected Chester Carlson's new photographic process in 1930 because it did not relate to their paradigm of photography. One company did have foresight – the Xerox Corporation.

Most of us can become better at generating new solutions if we:

- challenge our own paradigms;
- listens to others with a totally different view (they probably have a different paradigm);
- listen to our own intuition and have faith in our own absurd ideas rather than suppress them.

If you cannot generate new solutions, keep your mind open to others' ways of doing thing and see if they are worth copying. IBM copied Apple's radical approach to enter the PC market; Wimpy copied McDonalds by becoming counter service rather than table service restaurants.

'Seeing is Believing' – our beliefs and perceptions about what is right or possible prevent us from exploring new solutions. Remember what happened to the frog and the pike!

(*Authors note*: The experiments quoted are 'classic' experiments which have been carried out in the past by behavioural scientists. Refs: The Frog – *Shaping Your Organisation's Future, Frogs, Dragons, Bees and Turkey Tails*, J. William Pfeiffer *et al.*, Pfeiffer & Co San Diego; The Pike – Eden Ryl, Ramic Productions Film, *Grab Hold of Today*. I assure you that I have neither boiled frogs, nor starved pike to death ⇁ MH.

Allow me to introduce myself

Know thyself
CHILO (BC 560)

I Can Do That! is about **you** This five-minute activity will help **you** to think about your past and future life, both at work and at home.

Few of us are fortunate enough to have our own personal crest, so here is an opportunity for **you** to design yours!

Complete the *I Can Do That!* crest on page 8, using the following guidelines:

Draw a picture in each of the sections to illustrate:

Section 1 *How I like to spend my leisure time*
Section 2 *Something I did recently that I'm really proud of*
Section 3 *My greatest professional skill*
Section 4 *My greatest challenge for the next six months*
Banner *Write your own personal motto or slogan*

This simple activity can be very useful to help **you** to start finding the key to unlock the answer to who **you** are and who **you** want to be. Why not take it out of the book, or photocopy it and put it on the wall where you're planning to work on *I Can Do That!*

Self-esteem, stress and jobsearching

Worry gives a small thing a big shadow
SWEDISH PROVERB

Embarking on a jobsearch programme can be challenging, enjoyable and rewarding.

For many people the career and life planning, which is part of our job-searching process, is enlightening. It represents a removal of the blinkers – the first time they have looked at their own life, beyond the end of their nose! Jobsearching can also be very depressing because:

Jobsearches for positions in sales look like this:

NO	NO	NO	NO	NO	NO	NO	NO	NO	NO	
NO	NO	NO	NO	NO	NO	NO	NO	NO	NO	
NO	NO	NO	NO	NO	NO	NO	NO	NO	NO	**YES**

Jobsearches for positions in accounts look like this:

NO	NO	NO	NO	NO	NO	NO	NO	NO	NO	
NO	NO	NO	NO	NO	NO	NO	NO	NO	NO	
NO	NO	NO	NO	NO	NO	NO	NO	NO	NO	**YES**

Jobsearches for recent graduates look like this:

NO	NO	NO	NO	NO	NO	NO	NO	NO	NO	
NO	NO	NO	NO	NO	NO	NO	NO	NO	NO	
NO	NO	NO	NO	NO	NO	NO	NO	NO	NO	**YES**

Jobsearches for women-returners look like this:

NO	NO	NO	NO	NO	NO	NO	NO	NO	NO	
NO	NO	NO	NO	NO	NO	NO	NO	NO	NO	
NO	NO	NO	NO	NO	NO	NO	NO	NO	NO	**YES**

Jobsearches for administrators look like this:

NO	NO	NO	NO	NO	NO	NO	NO	NO	NO	
NO	NO	NO	NO	NO	NO	NO	NO	NO	NO	
NO	NO	NO	NO	NO	NO	NO	NO	NO	NO	**YES**

Whatever job you're searching for, jobsearches all look pretty similar! Sometimes there are more Nos, sometimes less. Since few of us are good at taking **NO**, it's hardly surprising that a number of jobsearchers begin their jobsearch with a burst of initial enthusiasm which then turns to anxiety, self-doubt and depression.

REDUNDANCY

Perhaps you have noticed that I have avoided the term
(redundant). A man cannot actually be redundant.
He can be wrong for a job, his job can disappear from beneath
him, his firm may have to contract for financial reasons,
but I submit that he cannot actually be redundant. He is
a man fresh out of a job, and he is a man who needs to be
relocated in a new job. But he remains a man, not an empty
space where one once was.
(MALCOLM LEVENE, *The Observer*)

First let me apologise to women on Mr Levene's behalf – he seems to have failed to recognise their contribution to the workforce!

Whatever euphemisms people may use and whatever the organisational reasons, like 'downsizing', 'financial contraction' or 'mergers', in reality, the expression we all use as shorthand to describe what's happened is to say 'S/he's been made redundant'.

My father was made redundant after 38 years as a coal miner, my brother-in-law was made redundant after eight years as a security guard, and I was made redundant after 12 years in management.

There can be few people who do not know someone in their close group of friends or relatives who has not been 'made redundant'. Only when it happens to you can you begin to have an inkling of the effect it can have on a person's life.

Those who trivialise redundancy with statements like, 'Well of course if you haven't been made redundant at least once in your career, then you haven't been where the action is', probably haven't been there, or they'd be more sensitive.

Now I'm not going to insult you by offering trite and facile advice like 'Remember tomorrow's another day' and 'Keep smiling and it'll all come good soon'.

It might be worth recognising, however, that you're not alone. You're not the only person who feels like they've received a kick in the ego from a size 12 boot. Common feelings are:

- **SHOCK** – not being able to appreciate what's happening.
- **DENIAL** – it's not really happening.
- **ANGER** – why me?

- **LOST SELF-IMAGE** – I've failed, my job has gone. I'll never get another.
- **LOW SELF-ESTEEM** – I'm worthless, I'm insecure.
- **LOSS** – of direction, colleagues, security and all of the 'comforts' which come from regular work.
- **REJECTION** – by the previous employer, by potential employers when they don't acknowledge applications, and by friends when they don't return phone calls.
- **STIGMA** – how do my friends and neighbours now feel about me? What will the children tell their school friends?
- **LACK OF CONTROL** – what if I contact all of my friends, identify lots of opportunities, make lots of applications, get interviewed, but still don't get a job?

Now all of that has cheered you up hasn't it! But you **can** take control. **You now have a job**. Your job is finding a new job, because it's unlikely that the job is going to come looking for you.

The success of your jobsearch will depend on both the quality and quantity of your efforts. Working through the activities in the book will help with the quality. You are in charge of the quantity, the number of hours you commit. Don't expect the telephone to start ringing just because you've sent your CV to three or four recruitment agencies.

Persistence does pay off. It is generally believed that when they get back into work most people get a job with more responsibility, greater job satisfaction and a higher salary than their previous job.

JOBSEARCHING IS STRESSFUL

Changing jobs is regarded by 'experts' as being one the most stressful things in our lives.

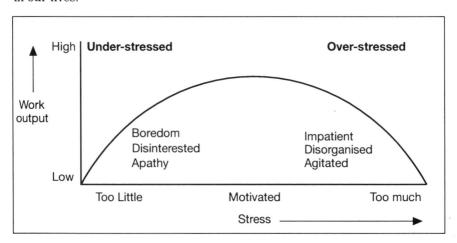

Figure 1

In day-to-day life we need an amount of stress. To an extent the more stress we have then the better we work (see Figure 1). In other words, you need to **strike the balance, between challenge and having the resources to cope**.

TO AVOID BECOMING OVER-STRESSED

- Take a proper break for lunch.
- Have a relaxation break for five minutes every hour or so.
- Take twenty minutes exercise three times per week.
- Manage your time – organise your day so that you can spend some time relaxing with your friends and family.
- Have clear objectives – both long- and short-term ones – of what you want to achieve.

LOOK OUT FOR SIGNS OF BEING OVER-STRESSED

LEVEL 1
Over energetic, over enthusiastic, over conscientious, overworked, feeling of uncertainty, doubts about coping.

Look out for:
Too busy to take time off, not knowing when to stop jobsearching, too little time spent with partner/family, frustrated with results.

LEVEL 2
Irritation, tiredness, anxiety, feeling of stagnation, blaming others.

Look out for:
Complaints about other people, unable to cope with pressure of handling a number of things at once, working long hours, not managing time efficiently.

LEVEL 3
General discontent, increasing anger/resentment, lowering of self-esteem, growing guilt, lack of emotional commitment, apathy.

Look out for:
Not enjoying life, extreme exhaustion, reduced commitment to jobsearching, reduced commitment to home.

LEVEL 4
Withdrawl, illness, feelings of failure, extreme personal distress.

Look out for:

Avoiding jobsearching activities, avoiding contact with other people, reluctance to communicate, isolation, physical illness, inability to get to sleep/early waking, alcohol or drug abuse.

IF YOU BECOME OVER-STRESSED

The following list offers some suggestiions on how you can cope with stress.

- Try to analyse the problem logically, brainstorm solutions and pick the best options.
- Ask other people for advice.
- Spend time talking to other people (about anything!).
- Spend some time on your hobby.
- Take a weekend break.
- Eat proper, regular meals.
- Take some strenuous exercise.
- Reduce your intake of caffeine and alcohol.
- Make love with your partner.
- Indulge yourself in a hot bath, sauna or a massage.
- Socialise with friends.
- Pour out your problems to a good friend.
- Write all of your frustrations down on a piece of paper and then tear it up into the tiniest pieces you can.
- Have a good cry or a good shout in the privacy of your home.
- Be creative: Write poetry, sing, play a musical instrument.
- Start writing a book!

If it all seems as if it is becoming too much, the Samaritans will lend an ear – the number is in your telephone directory. Other useful numbers can be found in the appendix.

Your local GP can also help. Indeed, many surgeries now have nurses who have received special training in counselling skills. They can be enormously useful in helping you to re-direct yourself.

Remember that you're not on your own. Your friends and family love and respect you, not for some job title you once held, but for the person you are.

Taking stock of my position

Instead of saying that man is the creature of circumstance, it would be nearer the mark to say that man is the architect of circumstance. It is character which builds an existence out of circumstance. From the same materials one man builds palaces, another hovels; one warehouses, another villas; bricks and mortar are mortar and bricks until the architect can make them something else.

THOMAS CARLYLE

In this activity, which is in two parts, you will think about your life from the time you were born through to the time of your death. Most people find these exercises extremely powerful and enlightening.

If someone close to you has died recently, you may feel uncomfortable thinking about death and may wish to come back to this exercise at a later date. Other people have found, however, that the closeness of their loss has made the exercise even more meaningful.

Part I

0

_____

●   ●

The zero over the left dot represents your birth. Write the year you were born below it.

At what age do you think you will die? This is a difficult question but try to answer. Above the dot on the right of the line indicate your age at the time of your death. Write the year of your death below the dot.

Now put an 'x' on the line to show where you are now, between your birth and your death.

Look at your `Life Line'.

What are your thoughts about the time that already has passed? What are your thoughts about the time that you have left? **What are the three most important things you want to do in the next ten years?** Write them below:

Goal A _____

_____

Goal B _____

_____

Goal C _____

_____

Part II

It sounds morbid, but writing your obituary can help you to think clearly about your past and future life.

Write *two* obituaries for yourself: one if you had died yesterday and another if you were to die ten years from now.

You can:

- do the activity alone.
- prepare your obituaries alone and then share them with your partner or a friend,
- work with your partner or a friend to prepare obituaries for each of you.

The next page contains an outline of subjects you may want to include. This outline is intended to stimulate your thinking; modify the format if you wish.

OBITUARIES

Complete the following sentences to write your own obituaries:

If I had died yesterday ...

(Name) _____ died _____ at the age of _____. He/she was working on

becoming _____ (Name) _____ had always dreamed

of _____. He /she had just completed _____. The thing

he/she always wanted to do, but never did was_____. (Name)_____

will be remembered for _____. People will miss most _____

_____.

He/she is survived by _____. The funeral will be _____

_____. (Other information)_____

_____.

If I were to die in 10 years' time ...

(Name) _____ died _____ at the age of _____. He/she was working on

becoming _____ (Name) _____ had always dreamed

of _____. He /she had just completed _____. The thing

he/she always wanted to do, but never did was_____. (Name)_____

will be remembered for _____. People will miss most _____

_____.

He/she is survived by _____. The funeral will be _____

_____. (Other information)_____

How do they compare? How will you make your '10 Years From Now' come true?

My finances

A wise man will make more opportunities than he finds.

FRANCIS BACON

For most people, their salary is their major form of income, yet many people identify their salary requirements in a totally subjective way. Often based on what recruitment ads say, we ignore the ones on lower salaries and notice only higher ones. We notice what contemporaries earn, what the next door neighbour earns, what our brother/sister earns, what our partner earns, etc., with little recognition of what **our** needs are!

If personal budgeting skills are one of your great strengths then this activity may be unnecessary. Others will find it very useful!

The exercise will help you to plan your finances and identify your Target Minimum Salary, i.e., 2 x outgoings total, from the six monthly Financial Planner, less any annual income.

If you are unemployed and are now the Managing Director of 'The Me Corporation' then you **must** do this exercise. After all, you wouldn't want to be employed by a company that didn't do proper financial planning, would you?

Gather together your bank statements, details of mortgage/rent, HP payments etc., and use the six-monthly Financial Planner (on page 19), to summarise your anticipated income and outgoings for the first month (use pencil).

Now repeat the exercise making your forecasts so that you build up a picture for the six-month period – this is a realistic period for many jobsearches.

Repeat the exercise at the end of the month and write how much you have spent in the 'actual' column. How are you doing against your budget? Do you need to re-forecast?

By carrying out this exercise you'll be able to anticipate those months when the gas bill, TV licence, car tax and car insurance all arrive at the same time! Also, you'll probably realise that with effective budgeting you can still indulge yourself in some of life's luxuries.

Six-monthly financial planner

BUDGET PERIOD _____ 199____ **TO** _____ 199____

(This form should be photocopied and enlarged)

Month												
Budget vs Actual	Budget £	Actual £	Budget £	Actual £	Budget £	Actual £	Budget £	Actual £	Budget £	Actual £	Budget £	Actual £
INCOME: Net Salaries												
Dividends Interest												
Other												
INCOME: TOTAL												
OUTGOINGS: Mortgage/Rent												
Loans/HP/Credit												
Household Services												
Insurances												
Transport												
Job Search												
House/Garden												
Food												
Holidays												
Social												
Dependants												
Personal												
Other												
OUTGOINGS: TOTAL												
Bank Opening Balances												
Bank Closing Balances												

INCOME
Net Salaries = Salary. Self/Partner. Redundancy payments. Unemployment Benefit. Social Security payments.
Other = Tax Refunds. Inheritance. Sale of Assets. Bonuses.
OUTGOINGS
Mortgage/Rent = Regular Amount. Endowment assurance.
Loans/HP/Credit Cards = Total repayments. Items being paid off monthly.
Household Services = Water Rates. Council Tax. Gas. Electricity. Telephone. TV Licence/rent. Utilities.
Insurance = House & Buildings. Life Policies. Medical. House contents. Car(s). Accident/Disability. Pensions.
Transport = Car purchase. Fuel. Service/MOT. Road Tax. AA. RAC subs. Repairs/Tyres.Bus/Rail fares.

Jobsearch = Secretarial services. Equipment. Postage. Paper/Journals. Phone calls (Free at Jobclub if 6mths + unemployed).
House/Garden = Maintenance. Alterations. DIY. Central heating. Furniture, etc. Garden tools. Plants. Sheds/fences.
      Domestic appliance maintenance/replacement.
Food = Family. Guests. Pets.
Holidays = Fares. Insurance. Hotels. Car Hire. Entertainment. Gifts.
Social = Dining Out. Entertainment. Clubs/Equipment.
Dependants = Allowances. School Fees. Gifts. Maintenance payments.
Personal = Clothes. Hobbies. Gifts. Church/Charity. Medical. Dental/Optician. Professional subs. fees.
Other = Bank Charges. Income Gains Tax (if taxable). Contingencies.

FINANCIAL TIPS

These are primarily intended for unemployed jobsearchers but others may find the advice useful.

- Talk to your bank manager (check first to make sure there won't be a charge). They are financial experts and will be able to offer advice on budgeting and also advise on ways to invest a redundancy payment. In this transitory period of your life, however, be very wary of investments where you can't get your money back quickly and without penalty. Longer-term investments can be looked at when you've settled into the new job.

- Look for the simple ways of saving money – a magazine could cost you £2.00 in the newsagents, but can be read free at the local library. Going for a walk costs nothing and can be a great opportunity to think and plan.

- Talk to an independent financial adviser from a reputable company (beware, for many 'independent' and 'financial advisers' are misnomers, since they will have a vested interest in earning a sales commission). Talking to a financial adviser will help you to review your total financial picture e.g., would it be advisable to take out additional short-term life assurance, now that you aren't covered by the company's policy? Is your Will up to date? Should I leave my pension in my ex-company's fund or take a Personal Pension Plan?

- Contact your Inland Revenue Office – you may qualify for a refund.

- Sign-on at the Job Centre and ask about benefits you are entitled to receive, including any job clubs, adult training and community work opportunities available. If you have been out of work for some time, an up-to-date reference from one of these organisations can be worth its weight in gold.

- Some money-saving techniques can also generate a small income e.g., my daughter Alison is keen on crafts, so she makes jewellery and sells it at craft fairs. I like to keep up-to-date with Management Education, so I teach on the Open University Business School Courses ('Teaching is learning twice'!). My friend Roland is keen on keep-fit so he trained as a 'Step' aerobics instructor. Now he gets free membership to his health-club and his earnings from a weekly class subsidise his other hobbies.

- Clear out your loft and your garage – a trip to a car-boot sale as a seller can be enormous fun and you'll be amazed at what people will buy! But don't be unrealistic with your prices – remember people are looking for bargains.

- Lock away your credit cards! Being unemployed can be extremely expensive. Suddenly you have time on your hands and on your strolls down the high street you'll see lots of bargains you'd never seen before (you were at work!) – you didn't need them then, so do you really need them now?!

Lock away your credit cards!

- If you have to sell a 'luxury' asset (e.g., your classic car, a boat or a piece of jewellery) then plan the sale well in advance so that you can obtain a realistic price. If you have to sell quickly, in desperation, you may accept a much lower price. Not only will you lose out financially, but it will depress you as well!

DEBTS

- Tackle the problem immediately.
- Water, gas, telephone and electricity companies, etc., will often accept small instalments, as will credit card companies
- Contact the Social Security Hotline for free advice in office hours. Freephone:

0800 666 555 English
0800 289 188 Urdu
0800 521 360 Punjabi

When you have predictable and regular income, you can often get away without paying too much heed to the outgoings!

When income is substantially reduced, with no immediate prospect of improvement, what you can take control of is the management of your outgoings.

Assessing my needs and wants in life

Ethics, too, are nothing but reverence for life. That is what gives me the fundamental principle of morality, namely, that good consists in maintaining, prompting and enhancing life and that destroying, injuring and limiting life are evil.

ALBERT SCHWEITZER

Step 1

Look at the statements below. Tick the **seven** that are most important to you.

To feel I have stretched myself/fulfilled my potential. ☐

To make worthwhile things or provide a valued service. ☐

To be a successful parent. ☐

To be respected and acknowledged at work and home. ☐

To have a secure and untroubled life. ☐

To travel the world/Europe/country. ☐

To have as much pleasure as possible. ☐

To have no regrets in life. ☐

To enjoy love and companionship. ☐

To earn as much money as possible. ☐

To work overseas. ☐

To be free of other people's demands. ☐

To be a successful partner to my spouse. ☐

To do what I believe to be my duty. ☐

To help people less fortunate than I am. ☐

To become an acknowledged expert. ☐

To have power over other people. ☐

To become as famous as possible. ☐

Others. ☐

Step 2

Make notes of how you might be able to adapt your life to make sure that you are achieving your needs and wants.

Now rank those seven from most important (1) to least important (7).

1 _____

2 _____

3 _____

4 _____

5 _____

6 _____

7 _____

Keep these in mind when searching for your **ideal** job.

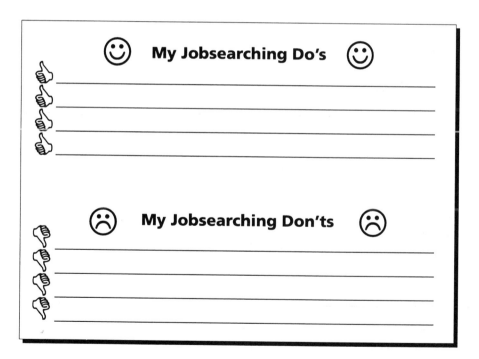

Use these notepads to summarise your learning points as you complete activities in *I Can Do That!*

My own skills and knowledge

A man's best friends are his ten fingers.

ROBERT COLLYER

If I asked you to list your skills and the knowledge that might be useful in your new job, in the box below, you'd probably say, 'there's far too much room'!

Try it anyway

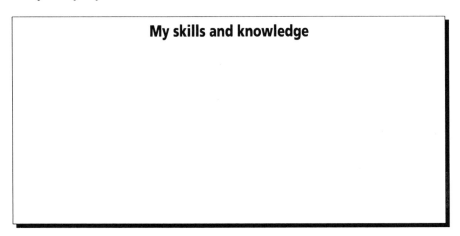

My skills and knowledge

What you have just listed is the tip of the iceberg.

You might say *'I've been too busy bringing up a family for the past 10 years to develop any new skills'*, or, *'I've been too busy hitting sales targets ...'* or, *'Studying for my degree ...'* to build up additional knowledge.

As we go through life, we develop skills and knowledge, either wittingly or unwittingly.

In this activity you will identify the skills and knowledge you have built up through **your** life so that you can identify the **Transferable Skills and Knowledge** to take into your new job.

Look at the three Skills Banks on the following pages and highlight or tick the skills you believe you have, are good at and enjoy doing. Then complete the 'Knowledge Reserves Exercise' on the next page. These exercises do take some time to complete. Do some initial work and then come back to them. Brainstorm with your partner or a close friend. It is worthwhile!

Your Transferable Skills and Knowledge Bank is the vault containing the currency to obtain your next job.

As you work through these activities keep thinking of specific examples and how you can expand from the 'general' to the 'specific'. For example if one of your skills is 'writing', then a good example might be that report you did for Senior Management which swayed a board meeting or the short story you had published.

Time invested on this activity will reap its rewards when you **write your CV, apply for jobs and attend interviews**. You will find that you can easily and quickly identify those top skills and knowledge that you have and, importantly, articulate them to a potential employer, whether in writing or at an interview.

SKILLS BANK

My transferable skills in dealing with people

I am good at and enjoy:

accepting	discovering	informing	pioneering	setting goals	using
acting	displaying	initiative	planning	sewing	washing
achieving	dissecting	inspecting	playing	shaping	winning
addressing	dramatising	inspiring	preparing	showing	working
administering	drawing	instructing	presenting	singing to	writing
advising	driving	integrating	problem-solving	sketching	
amusing	empathising	interpreting	processing	speaking	
analysing	empowering	interviewing	promoting	studying	
arbitrating	encouraging	investigating	protecting	summarising	
arranging	enforcing	judging	providing	supervising	
assessing	enthusing	keep fit	publicising	supplying	
auditing	establishing	leading	purchasing	symbolising	
budgeting	estimating	learning	questioning	synergising	
building	evaluating	lecturing	raising	synthesising	
caring	examining	listening	reasoning	systematising	
chairing	experimenting	maintaining	recommending	taking	
charting	explaining	making	reconciling	taking	
checking	expressing	inventories	recording	instructions	
classifying	financing	managing	recruiting	talking	
coaching	fixing	manipulating	referring	teaching	
communicating	following	mediating	rehabilitating	team-building	
conducting	founding	meeting	relating	telephoning	
consolidating	gathering	memorising	remembering	telling	
consulting	giving	mentoring	repairing	tending	
controlling	guiding	miming to	reporting	testing	
conversing	handling	modelling	representing	tolerating	
co-ordinating	having	monitoring	researching	ambiguity	
coping	responsibility	motivating	resolving	training	
counselling	heading	negotiating	responding	translating	
creating	healing	observing	restoring	treating	
cultivating	helping	offering	retrieving	trouble-	
debating	identifying	operating	risking	shooting	
deciding	problems	organising	scheduling	tutoring	
defining	illustrating	originating	screening	umpiring	
delivering	imagining	overseeing	selecting	understanding	
detailing	implementing	painting	self-	understudying	
detecting	improving	performing	understanding	undertaking	
developing	improvising	persuading	selling to	uniting	
ädiagnosing	increasing	photographing	sensing	updating	
directing	influencing	piloting	serving	upgrading	

SKILLS BANK
My transferable skills in dealing with things

I am good at and enjoy:

achieving	displaying	implementing	playing	scheduling	upgrading
adapting	disproving	improving	precision	sculpting	using
addressing	dissecting	improvising	predicting	selecting	utilising
administering	distributing	informing	preparing	selling	washing
analysing	drawing	innovating	prescribing	sensing	weaving
arranging	driving	inspecting	printing	separating	weighing
assembling	editing	integrating	problem-solving	serving	winning
auditing	eliminating	interpreting	processing	setting	woodworking
building	emptying	inventing	programming	setting-up	working
carving	enforcing	investigating	projecting	sewing	writing
checking	establishing	judging	promoting	shaping	
chiselling	estimating	keeping	proof-reading	showing	
classifying	evaluating	lifting	protecting	sketching	
cleaning	examining	logging	providing	solving	
collecting	expanding	maintaining	publicising	sorting	
compiling	expediting	making	purchasing	studying	
completing	experimenting	inventories	raising animals	summarising	
composing	extracting	managing	reading	supervising	
conserving	fashioning	manipulating	realising	supplying	
consolidating	feeding	manufacturing	reasoning	symbolising	
constructing	filing	massaging	receiving	synergising	
controlling	financing	memorising	recommending	synthesising	
cooking	finishing	metalworking	reconciling	taking	
co-ordinating	fixing	minding	re-constructing	taking	
crafting	forecasting	modelling	recording	instructions	
creating	founding	monitoring	recruiting	tending	
cultivating	gathering	motivating	reducing	testing and	
cutting	generalising	moulding	referring	proving	
deciding	generating	navigating	rehabilitating	tolerating	
delivering	generalising	observing	remembering	ambiguity	
designing	getting	obtaining	rendering	training animals	
detecting	giving	offering	repairing	transcribing	
determining	growing plants	operating	reporting	translating	
developing	hammering	ordering	representing	treating	
devising	handling	organising	researching	trouble-	
diagnosing	having	originating	resolving	shooting	
digging	responsibility	overseeing	responding	tutoring	
directing	heading	painting	restoring	typing	
disassembling	identifying	photographing	retrieving	understanding	
discovering	problems	piloting	reviewing	undertaking	
dispensing	illustrating	planning	salvaging	unifying	

SKILLS BANK

My transferable skills in dealing with concepts and information

I am good at and enjoy:

accounting	diagnosing	identifying	painting	restoring	transcribing
adapting	digging	problems	perceiving	retrieving	translating
administering	discovering	illustrating	piloting	reviewing	treating
analysing	displaying	imagining	planning	risking	trouble-
animating	disproving	implementing	predicting	scheduling	shooting
anticipating	dissecting	improving	preparing	searching	typing
ascertaining	distributing	improvising	prescribing	selecting	updating
assembling	diverting	increasing	prioritising	selling	understanding
assessing	dramatising	influencing	problem-solving	sensing	undertaking
auditing	drawing	initiating	processing	separating	unifying
budgeting	editing	innovating	programming	sequencing	uniting
calculating	eliminating	inspecting	projecting	setting-up	upgrading
charting	enforcing	installing	promoting	shaping	using
checking	establishing	instituting	proof-reading	sharing	utilising
classifying	estimating	integrating	protecting	sketching	verbalising
collecting	evaluating	interpreting	providing	solving	visualising
compiling	examining	inventing	publicising	sorting	weighing
completing	expanding	investigating	purchasing	storing	winning
composing	experimenting	judging	questioning	studying	working
computing	explaining	keeping	raising	summarising	writing
conceptualising	expressing	learning	reading	supplying	
conserving	extracting	logging	realising	symbolising	
consolidating	filing	maintaining	reasoning	synergising	
constructing	forecasting	making	receiving	synthesising	
controlling	formulating	managing time	recommending	systematising	
copying	founding	manipulating	reconciling	taking	
creating	gathering	mediating	recording	instructions	
deciding	generalising	memorising	reducing	telling	
decision-making	generating	modelling	referring	tending	
defining	getting	monitoring	relating	testing and	
delivering	giving	observing	remembering	proving	
designing	guiding	obtaining	reporting	thinking	
detecting	handling	operating	representing	logically	
determining	having	ordering	researching	tolerating	
developing	responsibility	organising	resolving	ambiguity	
devising	hypothesising	originating	responding	training	

Now that you have completed these Skills Banks, asterisk your 'Top Ten' on each page.

MY KNOWLEDGE RESERVES

It would be impossible to list an encyclopaedia of knowledge for you to use as a checklist, but **thinking about different times in your life should trigger you to remember knowledge you have acquired.**

Complete the chart below with subjects you know something about and enjoy.

Knowledge I have gained from:

School/College/ University e.g., Basic French	Work e.g., Auditing principles	Courses/ Apprenticeships/ Military e.g., Safety regulations
Reading: Books/ Newspapers/Magazines e.g., *Car Values*	**Computers/Video** e.g., Career planning	**Trial & Error/Self Study** e.g., Marketing Principles

Activity 7

My personality

People have one thing in common; they are all different
ROBERT ZEND

Psychologists will probably argue for as long as people tread the earth as to whether our personality is 'caught' or 'taught' – whether we inherit it from our parents, or it develops as a result of our interaction with our environment. Whichever way we get it, we all have one! This exercise will help you to learn more about yours and about your personality 'type'

Each of the paired blocks below contains two groups of words. Consider each block in turn and decide which list of words describes you best. There are no right answers and none of the groups of words are 'better' than any other. Do not choose how you would like to behave, but how you know you behave. You will probably find that some words in each of the paired blocks apply to you. Don't sit on the fence; choose which list is the better description of you. When you have made your choice circle the appropriate letter.

Circle your choice. Are you ...

E or I

E	I
Sociable	Composed
Expressive	Avoid crowds
Think out loud	Like one-to-one meetings
Like socialising in groups	Enjoy your own company
Uninhibited	Keep thoughts to yourself
Enjoy interacting with people	Entertain close friends in intimate groups

S or N

S	N
Factual	Conceptual
Operate from experience	Look for the 'big picture'
Practical	Innovative
Down to earth	Consider options
Pay attention to details	Enjoy new ideas
Make few errors	Future-oriented
Realistic	

T		F	
	Logical		Genuine
	Rational		Relationship-centred
	Objective		Harmonious
	Analytical		Base decisions on personal values
	Fair		Compassionate
	Seek knowledge		Loyal and supportive

J or P

J		P	
	Determined		Flexible
	Plan		Spontaneous
	Organised		Consider all of the options
	Purposeful		Adaptable
	Set goals		Enjoy variety
	Decide quickly		Like to keep options open

Now write the four letters you circled here (e.g., ENTJ) __ __ __ __

This activity is based on basic personality characteristics and in the following pages you'll find a summary of your profile.

Clearly there are more than 16 (the number of combinations) 'kinds of people' in the world and I suggest that you now **personalise your profile by crossing out words or expressions which do not describe you and using a highlighter pen, pick out those that are definitely you.**

This unique profile of you will be useful in helping you to communicate to employers the strengths that you can contribute to their organisation.

The section 'Others May Be Uneasy With', in the profiles on the following pages, has been left blank. Try to see yourself the way others may see you and complete this section yourself in order to build a balanced view of your strengths and limitations. Discuss your profile with your partner or a close friend.

Author's note: No explanation is offered here of the meanings of each of the letters associated with the 'questionnaire'. People trained in administering personality evaluations know what the letters stand for. It is far beyond the scope of this book to train you as a user of personality profiling instruments. Also, because of the simplicity of the exercise, it does not claim to be as accurate as the lengthy personality profiles carried out by psychologists. If you have access to this facility you will find it extremely useful. The type 'descriptors' e.g., Fieldmarshal, are taken from *Please Understand Me* by David Kiersy, an excellent reference, as is *Life Types* by Sandra Hirsh, if you wish to find out more about personality types (see appendix).

INTP – The Architect

STRENGTHS

Creative

Handles change easily

Theoretical

Researches objectively

Idealist

Likes solving complex problems

Imaginative

Innovative

An 'idea' person

Has intellectual insight

AS A LEADER

Prefers to organise things, not people

Writes letters

Enjoys designing change

Enjoys pioneering concepts and ideas

Provides vision and scope

AS A TEAM MEMBER

Accepts the challenge of complex
concepts

Is the 'idea' person

Is able to act as a reviewer of a project

Can incorporate change at any time

Offers creativity and innovation to a
project

AT WORK

Needs quiet with occasional privacy

Wants flexibility

Enjoys challenges

Likes an unstructured workspace

Workspace may be cluttered

AT HOME/WITH FRIENDS

Is earnest and devoted parent

Uses low-key discipline

Likes a quiet home setting

Works at play

Prefers thinking games, i.e., bridge,
chess etc.

OTHERS MAY BE UNEASY WITH

WHEN COMMUNICATING

Prefers written rather than verbal
contact

Wants to discuss the 'big picture'

Likes discussing concepts and ideas

Can be hypothetical and verbose

Enjoys one-to-one contact

SUMMARY

Original

Future-oriented

Inquisitive

Speculative

Reserved

Global thought

Analytical

Independent

Determined

Uses abstract ideas

ENTP – The Inventor

STRENGTHS

Alert to new possibilities

Entrepreneurial

Looks for better ways

Adapts to change

Enjoys learning new skills

Politically astute

Conceptual

Tactical

Like problem-solving

AS A LEADER

Is sociable and outgoing

Encourages innovation and creativity in others

Is open to constructive criticism

Relies on others to handle details

Develops models

AS A TEAM MEMBER

Makes strong initial contributions

Acts as the 'detonator' for the team

Incorporates new ideas

Sees the project reflected through people

Sees relationships between means and ends

AT WORK

Works best with independent people

Wants flexible management and guidelines

Needs challenge and reward for risk-taking

Enjoys group activities and gatherings

Likes 'start-ups' or re-organisations

AT HOME/WITH FRIENDS

Is high-spirited and outgoing

Enjoys group activities and gatherings

Wants a lively environment

Has an 'open door' policy

Likes flexible relaxation time

OTHERS MAY BE UNEASY WITH

WHEN COMMUNICATING

Is quick and verbal

Enjoys debate

Is an interesting conversationalist

Is a motivating speaker

Is stimulated by new information

SUMMARY

Understands people

Enjoys new projects

Open-minded

Communicative

Curious and interested

Likes variety and action

Instinctive

Analytical

Enjoys a challenge

Enthusiastic and energetic

INTJ – The Scientist

STRENGTHS

Highly practical

Systematic

Individualistic

Mentally quick

Committed

Independent

Resolute

Visionary

Self-motivated

Firm

AS A LEADER

Conceptualises and designs work models

Organises ideas into action plans

Plans strategies for new projects

Is tough-minded and decisive

Instils drive in self and others to attain goals

AS A TEAM MEMBER

Pushes for removal of obstacles

Has organisational vision

Is able to systemise goals

Implements new ideas

Streamlines complicated tasks and procedures

AT WORK

Likes intellectual challenges

Needs privacy for reflection

Wants efficient systems and procedures

Requires a certain amount of autonomy

Prefers a free hand for making decisions

AT HOME/WITH FRIENDS

Combines business with pleasure

Seldom leaves relaxation time to chance

Prefers well-planned activities

Is loyal and caring

Promotes independence in children

OTHERS MAY BE UNEASY WITH

WHEN COMMUNICATING

Communicates with specific purposes in mind

Believes that if people 'see it' they will understand it

Is detached and factual

Collects information visually

Uses logical structure

SUMMARY

Highly practical

Systematic

Individualistic

Mentally quick

Committed

Detached

Independent

Determined

Visionary

Self-motivated

Stable

Logical

ENTJ – The Fieldmarshal

STRENGTHS

Enjoys being a leader

Provides structure

Highly analytical

Frank and to the point

Expects hard work

Sets high standards

Likes problem-solving

Admires strength in others

Uses helpful critiques

Prepares for all situations

AS A LEADER

Takes charge

Works for long-term goals

Follows structure and systems

Decisive and tough

Has priorities and deadlines

AS A TEAM MEMBER

Lays out a blueprint for success

Makes planning logical and workable

Accepts responsibility of explaining to
    others

Sees that the plan is fully implemented

Breaks project into elements

AT WORK

Wants to identify personally with the
    job

Prefers tough-minded colleagues

Prefers an orderly, controlled
    environment

Seeks both challenge and structure

Wants results to be valued

AT HOME/WITH FRIENDS

Organises and structures family events

Integrates family and career

Enjoys competition

Organises relaxation

Expects dedication and commitment
    from partners

OTHERS MAY BE UNEASY WITH

WHEN COMMUNICATING

Relies on the sixth sense

Looks for the 'structure' of information

Likes to debate an issue

Has a natural clarity of thought and speech

Is gifted with insights to language and
    its meaning

SUMMARY

Gregarious

Quick-witted

Controlled objectivity

Firm, yet fair

Efficient

Logical

Verbalises easily and well

Seeks challenge

Strategic

INFP – The Questor

STRENGTHS

Creative
Persuasive
Encourages others
Has a sense of timing
Intuitive with people

Is genuinely enthusiastic
Awareness of time/history
Is gifted with languate
A good listener
Is inspired by challenge

AS A LEADER

Prefers to facilitate rather than direct
Seeks out the self-starters
Subtle

Praises other people naturally
Is open to other people's ideas

AS A TEAM MEMBER

Emphasises need for group or
　　organisational values
Presents high ideals and a goal of
　　perfection

Stimulates co-operation
Senses the true needs of other
Is humanitarian

AT WORK

Works well alone
Prefers a company of high integrity
Needs time to reflect

Desires co-operative peers
Wants to be independent

AT HOME/WITH FRIENDS

Relates well to children
Allows others freedom and space
Is easygoing, flows with family needs

Schedules may be subject to change
Is protective of the home and family

OTHERS MAY BE UNEASY WITH

WHEN COMMUNICATING

Communicates best via the written word
Writes lyrically
Stresses importance of relationships

Moves people through use of words
Listens with sincere interest

SUMMARY

Idealist
Supporter of causes
Faithful
Searches for the truth
Noble

Honourable
Harmonious
Dedicated to duty
Gentle/polite
Committed

ENFP – The Reporter

STRENGTHS

Originates projects

Anticipates needs

Stimulates potential

Concentrates intensely

At ease with others

Appreciates others' input

A perceptive observer

Looks on the bright side

Gives people 'space'

Sees people's potential

AS A LEADER

Knows how to motivate people

Promotes harmony

Conveys the overall value of work to
others

Accepts new projects

Uses variety to stimulate others

AS A TEAM MEMBER

Brings enthusiasm and energy

Is a catalyst who brings people together

Initiates meetings and conferences

Gets things moving from the start

Provides new and interesting aspects
and ideas

AT WORK

Enjoys working with colleagues

Prefers an open, friendly atmosphere

Needs variety and challenge

Enjoys an optimistic, idea-oriented
workplace

Works best with warm, lively people

AT HOME/WITH FRIENDS

Is charming and gentle with others

Brings in surprise and pleasure

Is a devoted and flexible parent

Enjoys bringing people together

Seeks out unusual recreation

OTHERS MAY BE UNEASY WITH

WHEN COMMUNICATING

Is skilled with the written word

Stresses values

Wins trust through charm and flair

Listens intently

Involves other people in conversation

SUMMARY

Charismatic

Zest for life

Discerning

Dynamic

Impromptu

Energetic and enthusiastic

Convincing

Intuitive with people

Versatile

Imaginative

INFJ – The Author

STRENGTHS

Listens to others

Co-operative

Creative/innovative

Looks to the future

Determined

Puts integrity first

Consults with others

Patient in relationships

Gentle and accepting

Loyal

AS A LEADER

Is low key, yet determined

Matches people to the tasks

Wins co-operation from others

Supports causes and ideals

Inspires others to succeed

AS A TEAM MEMBER

Is an ambassador

Has insight into the needs of others

Works with integrity and consistency

Faces challenge to gain ideals

Helps others to achieve their goals

AT WORK

Needs solitude and room for
concentration

Seeks an easy-going environment

Likes room to be creative

Enjoys challenging and novel projects

Wants an organised and harmonious
setting

AT HOME/WITH FRIENDS

Is concerned about home comforts

Develops long-term relationships

Enjoys a variety of interests and pursuits

Is a congenial companion

Is subtle in expressing affection

OTHERS MAY BE UNEASY WITH

WHEN COMMUNICATING

Is an elegant communicator, both
written and oral

Prioritises the feelings of others

Considerate of others' views

Has a natural gift for language

Uses relationships as communication
values

SUMMARY

Considerate

Highly committed

Calm and sensitive

Harmonious

Diplomatic

Warm

Inspires others

Compassionate

Reserved

Accepts challenges

ENFJ – The Pedagogue

STRENGTHS

Inspirational
Asks for commitment
Stimulates loyalty
Communicates values
Tactful

Has high standards
Uses an orderly approach
Wins others' respect
Gains co-operation
Responsive

AS A LEADER

Assigns tasks based on peoples' needs
Promotes group participation
Concerned about the feelings of
colleagues

Prefers to know who is involved prior to
decisions
Likes to adhere to the plan once it is
underway

AS A TEAM MEMBER

Provides information about human issues
Relies on personal experiences and
information
Protects the ideas and values of the
organisation

Has an orderly approach
Maintains co-operation within the team

AT WORK

Desires an environment to benefit
everyone
Expects surroundings to be settled and
orderly
Likes a value-based, principled
organisation

Enjoys harmony among co-workers
Wants a social, yet professional, feeling

AT HOME/WITH FRIENDS

Is romantic and devoted
Likes involved and caring relationships
Values harmony in the home

Family and responsibilities come first
Is community/service-oriented

OTHERS MAY BE UNEASY WITH

WHEN COMMUNICATING

Is openly talkative and social
Generates group involvement
Uses values and traditions as examples

Learns through interrelations
Perceptive

SUMMARY

Loyal
Diplomatic
Harmonious
People-oriented
Expressive

Responsible
Idealist
Supportive
Communicative
Concerned
Expressive

ESFJ – The Seller

STRENGTHS

Gentle, yet firm
Fast, thorough worker
Quick to act
Promotes loyalty
Decisive

Unselfish with time
Excellent with people
Tirelessly assists others
Tactful with colleagues
Creates harmony

AS A LEADER

Leads through attention to individuals
Keeps people informed
Adds a 'personal touch'

Sets an example for hard work
Uses experience to support decisions
   and actions

AS A TEAM MEMBER

Promotes team efforts
Resolves conflicts
Is punctual and accurate with data

Respects rules and authority
Is in tune with the needs of
   people/employees

AT WORK

Likes goal-oriented colleagues
Prefers friendly, organised surroundings
Likes being where the action is

Needs colleagues who are appreciative
   and sensitive
Provides service within specified structure

AT HOME/WITH FRIENDS

Enjoys socialising and entertaining
Is the centre of an ordered family life
Is a provider for the future

Is warm, caring and committed
Is self-sacrificing and loyal

OTHERS MAY BE UNEASY WITH

WHEN COMMUNICATING

Is an entertaining conversationalist
Listens with understanding and
   sympathy
Appreciates others' viewpoints

Is a strong verbal communicator
Obtains information through the senses

SUMMARY

Gregarious
Supportive
Sympathetic
Co-operative
Popular

Respects tradition
Gracious
Personable
Conscientious
Helps friends

ISFJ – The Conservator

STRENGTHS

Uses resources wisely

Knowledgeable

Just and fair

Task-oriented

Works tirelessly

Considerate of others

Personalises data

Accepts responsibility

Plans ahead

Simplifies information

AS A LEADER

Is consistent and orderly

Sets priorities around people

Is focused and detailed

Uses personal influence discreetly

Preserves traditional rules and
procedures

AS A TEAM MEMBER

Is thorough and painstaking

Carries out detailed and routine tasks

Makes effective decisions and takes
action

Personalises the goals and projects

Provides stability and follow-through

AT WORK

Prefers a secure working environment

Needs time to be alone

Wants order and routines

Appreciates accurate and conscientious
colleagues

Enjoys direct physical involvement with
work

AT HOME/WITH FRIENDS

Is devoted to the family

Enjoys traditional family activities

Maintains impeccable surroundings

Relaxes when work is finished

Values personal belongings

OTHERS MAY BE UNEASY WITH

WHEN COMMUNICATING

Uses examples and samples to
communciate

Is direct and to the point

Is friendly and patient

Looks for clear-cut contrasts

Writes things down

SUMMARY

Sympathetic

Detailed and factual

Conscientious

Respects tradition

Sense of history

Impromptu

Down-to-earth

Sense of justice

Service-oriented

Meticulous with detail

Practical and organised

ESFP – The Entertainer

STRENGTHS

A keen observer
A 'do it' person
Optimistic
Enthusiast
Advocates harmony

Accepts people for who they are
Generous with time
Sociable
Understands most people

AS A LEADER

Handles crises well
Facilitates the interaction of people
Promotes good will and teamwork

Is attentive to the expectations of others
Encourages agreement and compromise

AS A TEAM MEMBER

Brings in enthusiasm and co-operation
Offers action and excitement
Does it now – doesn't linger

Takes account of the needs of people
Supports the organisation loyally

AT WORK

Likes an energetic, yet easy-going,
   atmosphere
Prefers to focus on present realities
Prefers adaptable and lively colleagues

Likes the centre of action to be around
   people
Wants attractive surroundings

AT HOME/WITH FRIENDS

Is generous to others
Enjoys a beautifully decorated home
Is sentimental and enjoys pleasing others

Is sociable and spontaneous
Likes a varied and busy day

OTHERS MAY BE UNEASY WITH

WHEN COMMUNICATING

Is a straightforward communicator
Uses a simple and sensitive approach
Enjoys talking

Stimulates conversation
Relates today's situations to people

SUMMARY

Open and outgoing
Pleasant
Co-operative
Positive and upbeat
Empathetic

People-oriented
Tolerant
Realistic
Quick to act
Adaptable

ISFP – The Artist

STRENGTHS

Receptive to others
Generous with time
Open-minded
Generates trust in others
Respects others' feelings

Unconditionally kind
Eternal optimist
Solves problems
Understanding and trusting

AS A LEADER

Praises and encourages
Monitors group performance
Is adaptable and co-operative

At hand in a crisis
Is able to utilise the strengths of others

AS A TEAM MEMBER

Is co-operative
Brings focus to people's needs
Understands the need for teamwork

Builds systems around productive people
Provides service to a project

AT WORK

Needs a private, unconfined space
Wants compatible colleagues
Desires flexibility to be productive

Likes an aesthetic work environment
Is concerned about people's actions

AT HOME/WITH FRIENDS

Enjoys private leisure time
Is personable and humorous
Takes time for simple pleasures

Needs to maintain relationships
Enjoys solitary pursuits

OTHERS MAY BE UNEASY WITH

WHEN COMMUNICATING

Is in tune with the needs of others
Prefers clam, controlled conversations
Looks for meaning in people's actions
and words

Listens, before speaking
Likes quiet, considerate colleagues

SUMMARY

Gentle and considerate
Quiet disposition
Has an inner intensity
Can act spontaneously
Is in touch with reality

Unpretentious
Sensitive to others
Artistic
Unassuming
Co-operative and balanced

ESTJ – The Administrator

STRENGTHS

Plans ahead

Declares views openly

Uses experience

Good organiser

Follows through

Meets deadlines

Prompt decision maker

Respects authority

Tough-minded

Manages and controls

AS A LEADER

Is direct and to the point

Applies past experiences to resolve
problems

Uses rewards with employees

Takes charge

Firm, yet open to ideas

AS A TEAM MEMBER

Works well with policies and procedures

Is effective at controlling time spent on
a project

Understands the importance of full
co-operation

Is prepared to act when called upon

Uses a systematic approach to a
challenge

AT WORK

Enjoys being in charge

Likes to work alongside dedicated
colleagues

Prefers defined projects

Prefers stable and predictable
surroundings

Likes to work with, and through, people

AT HOME/WITH FRIENDS

Is community-minded

Is prudent and conservative

My home is my castle

Mixes business with pleasure

Has strong family ties

OTHERS MAY BE UNEASY WITH

WHEN COMMUNICATING

Is an effective verbal communicator

Is a good sounding board for others

Is crisp and direct

Communicates with facts

Wants outlines rather than details

SUMMARY

Deals in reality

Goal-oriented

Responsible

Stable

Systematic

Conscientious

Organiser

Thorough

Decisive

Logical and objective

ISTJ – The Trustee

STRENGTHS

Knows the rules

Follows guidelines

Likes structure

Dependable

Accepts responsibility

Adapts to new routines

Takes charge

Team-oriented

Puts work before play

Meets deadlines

AS A LEADER

Sets the standard for others

Is goal-oriented and expects others to be

Controls resources and costs

Is direct and succinct

Supports existing systems, structures and
 standards

AS A TEAM MEMBER

Organises and plans

Follows schedules

Meets deadlines

Respects traditions and rules

Takes responsibility for the project

AT WORK

Plans the work and works to the plan

Wants details

Likes a task-oriented, quiet environment

Prefers involvement

Expects work to be orderly

AT HOME/WITH FRIENDS

Is trustworthy and dedicated

Committed to the family

Expects rules to be adhered to

Is a pillar of strength

Is conservative

OTHERS MAY BE UNEASY WITH

WHEN COMMUNICATING

Likes visuals – flow-charts, diagram and
 graphs, etc.

Direct and to the point

Is logical and sequential

Respects agendas

Relates to experience

SUMMARY

Thorough

Factual

Tangible

Consistent

Committed

Reliable

Reserved

Orderly

Systematic

Down-to-earth

ESTP – The Promoter

STRENGTHS

Straightforward

Handles risks

A negotiator

Initiates

Responds quickly

Results-oriented

Remembers data and facts

Takes action

Mediates problems

A realist

AS A LEADER

Is direct

Is attentive at meetings

Handles problems quickly

Takes charge in emergencies

Uses persuasion to speed things along

AS A TEAM MEMBER

Acts as a go-between in negotiations

Adapts to working with all types

Supports projects with data and facts

Is able to adapt to last minute changes

Likes being the trouble-shooter

AT WORK

Wants a minimal bureaucracy

Includes time for fun while working

Wants an attractive work environment

Likes to master technical problems

Desires result-oriented colleagues

AT HOME/WITH FRIENDS

Is active with friends and family

Enjoys both personal and group
  activities

Has wide outside interests

Is a fun-loving charmer

Likes impromptu projects and parties

OTHERS MAY BE UNEASY WITH

WHEN COMMUNICATING

Uses both oral and visual communication

Is personable and engaging

Enjoys discussing plans and operations

Likes a 'real' debate

Is perceptive of body language

SUMMARY

Easygoing

Prepared for action

Lively and quick

A realist

Resourceful

Spontaneous

Versatile

Entertaining

Persuasive

Alert

ISTP – The Artisan

STRENGTHS

Receptive to others
Calm in a crisis
Trusting
Fountain of knowledge
Dextrous

Has technical insight
Risk-taker
Trouble-shooter
Gets things done
Action-oriented

AS A LEADER

Wants subordinates to follow their
  example
Manages work and people with minimal
  controls
Is able to respond to emergencies

Likes people to build action groups
Seeks new ideas and methods

AS A TEAM MEMBER

Enjoys compiling relevant technical data
Has a sense of priority to achieve a goal

Is able to adapt to last minute changes
Will work within specific guidelines
Wants to be involved in new projects

AT WORK

Likes project-oriented operations
Likes to work with action-oriented
  people
Wants to be involved

Likes dealing with things rather than
  people
Prefers flexible rules and procedures

AT HOME/WITH FRIENDS

Is private and protective of family
Is responsive and realistic
Is attentive to the needs of others

Is relaxed and easy-going
Enjoys repairing things for the family

OTHERS MAY BE UNEASY WITH

WHEN COMMUNICATING

Likes talking to people one to one
Is direct, yet open with others
Seeks essential facts

Likes technical data
Learns by doing

SUMMARY

Reserved
Factual
Logical
Adaptable
Independent

Practical
Down-to-earth
Analytical
Prudent
Spontaneous

What do I want from my job?

He that hath a trade hath an estate; he that hath a calling hath an office of profit and honour.

BENJAMIN FRANKLIN

Q *Why Do You Go To Work?* **A** *To earn a living.* But it goes way beyond that. Money is important - but it isn't everything. Research has shown that, whilst earnings are important, people expect a good deal more from their jobs. A recent survey by the Industrial Society showed interest/enjoyment, job security and a sense of accomplishment were more important than basic pay for most people. You are not 'most people' though.

Study the following and rank them: **1** for the factor most important to you, **15**, for the factor least important to you.

Job Factor	My Importance Ranking: 1–15
Advancement opportunities	
Basic pay	
Credit for a job well done	
Flexible hours	
Fully utilising skills/talents	
Go ahead employer	
Having a say	
Interest/enjoyment	
Job security	
Learning new skills	
Physical working conditions	
Sense of accomplishment	
Skilled management	
Sufficient help/equipment	
Working for a boss you respect	

When you're jobsearching check to make sure that at least your top five job factors will be satisfied. Don't leap on the salary bandwagon. Yes, it is important but it's not everything.

Imagine you're a Personnel Manager in a small company. You love the close contact you have with everyone. Your boss, the Managing Director, trusts and respects the quality of your work and gives you a wide amount of latitude to make decisions. She gives you fair appraisals and makes sure that you're always being stretched a little, by involving you in lots of nice project work. You love your job.

A telephone call from a head-hunter and a couple of interviews land you a job on £3,500 per year more *and* a company car? Yippee! You're now the Compensation and Benefits Specialist for 'Huge International'. You're locked in an office on the 10th floor, surrounded by computer terminals, a library of policies and procedures and computer printouts. You rarely see your boss. You can do the job standing on your head. You're bored to tears. You're ready to leave after six months, but all of a sudden the jobs have evaporated!

As you identify potential job opportunities check, as far as you can, to make sure that your top five or six job factors will be satisfied – after all, you wouldn't want to be starting all over again in another six months would you?

WHY PEOPLE RESIGN – THE SIX MOST COMMON REASONS

There are six main reasons why people resign and more than just one of these reasons is usually involved.

- **Initial expectations mis-match:** The interviewer fails to describe the position accurately. Initial expectations do not match up to the reality of working.

- **Lack of communication:** Normal work pressures often make communication difficult. People may feel forgotten, they think they are being given the 'mushroom treatment', always kept in the dark while up to their waists in manure. Isolation or uncertainty breed insecurity, apathy and cynicism. People resign out of frustration.

- **Challenge:** People hate being in a rut, feeling that they have outgrown their job.

- **Lack of recognition:** How many times have you felt your hard work and commitment have not even been recognised, let alone rewarded?

- **Training and development:** If a person is not developing and being stretched within his or her job, then the company is providing a job rather than a career. Training adds 'value' to the individual. It also makes a person appreciate the company more. It shows the company has a commitment to its people.

- **Culture fit:** Every company has its own style or culture. Sometimes there is a mis-match between a person and the company's culture and the employee leaves.

How does your target company measure up to these points? Use the checklist below to assess its suitability. If you cannot tick all six, ask yourself if it's the right **company for you.**

Target Company Checklist

- **Expectations**
  Do I/they know what I'm/they are letting myself/themselves in for ☐

- **Communication**
  Are channels of communication obvious? Do they work? ☐

- **Challenge**
  Am I going to be stretched? ☐

- **Recognition**
  Will my contribution be recognised? ☐

- **Training and development**
  Will I get any? ☐

- **Culture**
  Do I like their style? Will I fit in? ☐

☺ **My Jobsearching Do's** ☺

👍 _____

👍 _____

👍 _____

👍 _____

☹ **My Jobsearching Don'ts** ☹

👎 _____

👎 _____

👎 _____

Use these notepads to summarise your learning points as you complete activities in _I Can Do That!_

Career/life interface

Occasionally in life there are those moments of unutterable fulfilment which cannot be completely explained by those symbols called words. Their meanings can only be articulated by the inaudible language of the heart.
MARTIN LUTHER KING, JR.

Jobsearching and career planning isn't something you can do in isolation. The decisions you make about your career impact on your life outside work, just as your activities outside work impact on your career, e.g., business travel is a normal part of organisational life. In considering a new job, you may want to determine how much travel is involved and what effect that will have on your personal and family life. Having to work shifts changes the pattern of people's lives completely.

At the same time, it may be necessary to make certain *compromises* between your career and personal development. Only you can decide exactly what compromises you are prepared to make.

No matter how challenging and satisfying a job is, it cannot meet all of your needs for personal growth and development. You have a rewarding life outside work as well. Successful people are usually well-balanced, with a number of outside interests. A full leisure and family life refreshes them to perform more effectively at work and allows them to bring a broader scope of vision to their jobs.

This activity enables you to review how well you balance the different areas of your life. You will then set yourself goals for how you want to balance your life in future.

The activity is in three steps.

Step 1

Imagine that the circle below is a 'pie' representing your life during the last year. Divide the pie into slices representing how you currently (or most recently when working) allocate(d) your **waking time** – into the 'slices' of your life. Use any division that is meaningful to you. Possible labels for your slices could be:

- attending church
- children
- community and professional activites
- continuing education
- education
- entertainment

- personal development
- physical fitness
- professional development
- reading
- relationships
- shopping

- financial management
- fun
- hobbies
- household maintenance
- spending time with friends
- sports
- watching TV
- work

The size of each slice should represent the amount of time you spend on each activity. For example, if you spend/spent half your waking hours on work, that should account for half of the circle.

My 'Life Pie' for the Last Year

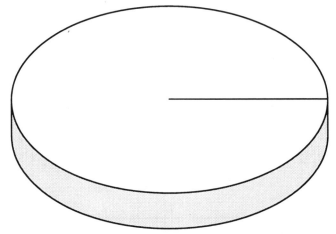

Step 2

Make a few notes as you answer these questions. Ask yourself.

- Am I satisfied with the way I balance my life?

- What parts are out of balance?

- What is the impact of this neglect on myself and those who are close to me?

- What activities do I spend too much time on and what can be done about it?

Now slice your 'ideal pie' as you would like to spend your time. To remind you, possible labels for your slices could be:

- attending church
- children
- community and professional activites
- continuing education
- education
- entertainment
- financial management
- personal development
- physical fitness
- professional development
- reading
- relationships
- shopping
- spending time with friends

- fun
- hobbies
- household maintenance

- sports
- watching TV
- work

My Ideal 'Life Pie'

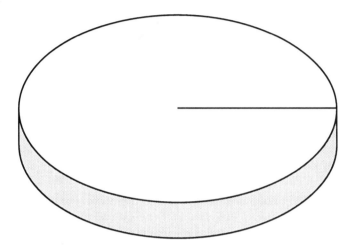

Step 3

Complete the Summary and Action Plan table. Write your aims in the left-hand column, e.g., *'I want to become fitter.* In the righthand column state what you intend to do about your aims, e.g., 'Join an aerobics club', to turn your aims, into achievable goals.

Time goals and action plan

Goals	Action Plan: What I'm going to do
I want to spend more time:	
I want to spend less time:	

My values

For anything worth having one must pay the price; and the price is always work, patience, love, self-sacrifice.

JOHN BURROUGHS

Values – what we care about – guide our actions and determine how we experience the world. Values change as we grow older, to reflect experiences and stages in our lives and careers. As children, our most important value may be winning the love of our parents. As we grow and mature, new values such as autonomy, achievement and the need of self-approval become important. Parenthood may shift the emphasis once again.

It can be easy to lose touch with what is important to us in the process of managing our day-to-day activities. Also, because many of us do not stop to reflect on our values, we fail to challenge the way we see the world.

Understanding your values can help you in:

● planning personal and career goals;

● selecting the kind of position and work to suit you;

● understanding the kind of people you most like to associate with;

● allocating your finances and time to achieve the greatest personal satisfaction.

This activity will help you to increase your awareness of what is most important to you and what you want out of your life and your career.

Read the values on page 55 If necessary, modify or re-write them to make them more meaningful to you. Add any values you feel are missing.

Mark each value in terms of its importance to you as high, medium or low (regardless of how well you are currently satisfying that value in your life). Try to allocate roughly one-third of the values to each category.

Complete the exercise as you think about these values right now. And remember, it's not what you think the world wants you to think, but it's what **you** value.

For most people the initial reaction is to place a high ranking on all of the values. Try to prioritise what are your most important and least important values at **this time in your life**.

WHAT I REALLY VALUE IN LIFE

	Importance		
	High	Medium	Low
Accomplishment: To achieve: to reach the top			
Affection: To obtain and share warmth, caring, companionship with family, friends, colleagues			
Affiliation: To be accepted and liked by others			
Autonomy: To direct my priorities and schedules			
Challenge: To have interesting, challenging work			
Competence: To be respected for my ability			
Expertise: To be a respected authority			
Family: To spend time with my family and to have meaningful relationships			
Growth: To maximise my full potential; to be constantly learning, changing and developing			
Health: Physical health, fitness			
Integrity: To have the courage of my convictions; to be honest, to uphold my beliefs			
Leadership: To influence and direct others			
Location: To live where I want to live			
Money: To be financially successful			
Pleasure: To have fun; to enjoy life and work			
Recognition: To have status and the respect of others			
Security: To achieve a secure financial situation			
Service: To help other people; to contribute to the well-being of others; to help improve society			
Spiritual: Inner harmony; to be at peace with myself and live by my moral and ethical beliefs			
Other values:			

When you have completed this section move to the next page.

SUMMARISING MY VALUES

Use this page to analyse how your values are currently being satisfied and what you must do in the future.

At this time in my life my five most important values are:

1. _____ 2. _____ 3. _____ 4. _____ 5. _____

My values which **must be** satisfied in my:

Working Life	Personal Life
• _____	• _____
• _____	• _____
• _____	• _____
• _____	• _____
• _____	• _____

Ways in which I may be able to achieve greater satisfaction of my values in my working life are:

_____

_____

_____

_____

Ways in which I may be able to achieve greater satisfaction of my values in my personal life are:

_____

_____

_____

_____

Activity 11

My life's achievements

They are able because they think they are able.
VERGIL

Do you keep a 'Brag Box', as my friend Tony calls it? My own is a bursting box file ... and as I'm writing this, I'm reminding myself that mine is overdue for updating! I can't think of a better name than the one Tony uses, so we'll call it a Brag Box! I'm talking about a collection point, for documents logging your achievements through life.

When you come to complete your CV, or find you've got one hour to fill in an application form in order to catch the post, you'll be glad of your Brag Box!

Do you keep a Brag Box?

Some of the things to include in your Brag Box (either as copies or originals) could be:

Birth Certificate	Exam Certificates
Marriage Certificate	Degree(s)
Children's Birth Certificates	Examples of your work
Passport (for No)	CV
Driving Licence	Personality and other evaluations

Membership Certificates for	Historical salary data
professional institutes	Performance rankings, e.g., sales figures
Licences to Practice	Special thank-you letter from your boss
Career evaluations	or the MD!
Testimonials	Sports Certificates
Appraisals	This book!

As well as the functional aspect, you'll find your Brag Box useful for cheering you up on a wet Tuesday afternoon, when you feel as if you've telephoned everyone in the world and 'They're all in meetings'! But don't get too lost down memory lane ... the meetings do end!

If you haven't got a brag box start one now!

Putting your brag box to work

Identifying your achievements will help you to realise that you have a wide variety of skills. You can use the information you develop in this exercise in CV presentation, completing application forms and job interviews.

Use the information in your Brag Box to help you to identify achievements you are proud of, pick:

- **4 from the past two years**
- **3 from the five year period before that**

Now think about the skills you used and what made your achievements so satisfying. The following phrases are often used in describing achievements:

Work Achievements

Improved productivity in _____ by _____.

Successfully convinced (my manager, subordinates, etc.) to _____.

Developed (introduced, designed, etc.) a new (method/system, etc.) for _____ resulting in _____.

Motivated subordinates by _____.

Detected a serious error in (a procedure, filing system, report etc.) and _____.

Improved technological process (service, etc.) by _____.

Successfully arranged and ran a meeting on _____.

Changed _____.

Improved quality control in _____ by _____.

Successfully arranged and ran a meeting on _____.

Initiated and implemented a (programme campaign, process, etc.) to _____.

Increased market share of _____.

Non-work achievements

Created (managed, ran, etc.) a fund-raising campaign for (name of charitable, athletic or artistic activity/group).

Successfully counselled, advised, helped a friend.

Organised (co-ordinated, etc.) a charitable drive.

Successfully renovated my home myself.

Established (acted as Secretary of) a professional association (social, athletic club, etc.)

Acted as a member of a committee or chaired a committee.

Did (oversaw) the decorations for _____.

As (a founding member of a local organisation) created a campaign to _____, successfully raised funds for _____ , etc.

Organised a day trip to _____,
for a group of _____ (mothers and toddlers).

Having identified your achievements complete the tables on the following pages. I have included an example to help you to start the process.

Example

Achievement	Skills used	What made the achievement satisfying
Co-ordinated sponsored run	Conceived the campaign	Managing
Enlisted six volunteers to assist in organising the campaign	Managing others	Planning the campaign
	Motivating others	Running meetings
Informed local newspaper to generate publicity	Planning	Contributing to something I believe in
Ran four meetings with volunteers	Organising	The results – £5,000!
Co-ordinated the volunteers by assigning tasks	Delegating tasks	Being recognised
Developed plan to go to the schools to inform people about the run and enlist volunteers	Running effective meetings	Being in the limelight
Got 200 people to participate in the run	Public relations – selling the campaign	
	Persuading people to participate	

ACHIEVEMENTS FROM THE PAST TWO YEARS

Achievement	Skills used	What made the achievemt satisfying
Achievement No 1		
Achievement No 2		
Achievement No 3		
Achievement No 4		

ACHIEVEMENTS FROM THE PAST SEVEN YEARS

Achievement	Skills used	What made the achievemt satisfying
Achievement No 5		
Achievement No 6		
Achievement No 7		

☺ **My Jobsearching Do's** ☺

_____
_____
_____
_____

☹ **My Jobsearching Don'ts** ☹

_____
_____
_____
_____

Use these notepads to summarise your learning points as you complete activities in *I can Do That!*

Seeking feedback from others

O wad some Pow'r the giftie gie us
To see oursels as others see us!
It wad frae mony a blunder free us,
And foolish notion.

ROBERT BURNS

All of the exercises so far have concentrated on self-analysis. The next step is to move from self-analysis to gather information about how other people see you. No matter how honest and thoughtful you have been, we all have blind spots! Others may point to weaknesses we are unaware of, or more commonly, strengths and abilities we have underestimated.

Clearly no two people will see you in exactly the same way. Nor is it true that other people will always see you more accurately than you see yourself. By talking to people whose opinion you value, you will develop a clearer picture of yourself.

Whose opinion do I value?

Write down the names of people whose opinions you value. These may be your:

- current manager
- colleagues
- friends
- partner

- previous manager
- subordinates
- family members
- neighbours

Ideally they
- have observed you in different situations
- know you well and how you react to different situations
- have your best interests at heart
- are perceptive

People whose opinions I value are:

_____

_____

_____

WHAT SORT OF THE FEEDBACK YOU WANT?

The feedback you solicit from each person will, of course, depend on your relationship with them.

Friends and family can provide you with important feedback in such areas as your interpersonal skills; decision-making style; communication skills; ease of social interaction; some of your personality characteristics; how well you plan; how well organised you are, etc.

Don't discount this feedback. If you can do something well at a party or at home, then the chances are that you could also do it well at work. Similarly, weaknesses seen at home are probably applicable to work as well. For example, if your partner tells you that you don't listen very well, or that you have difficulties managing your temper, then you probably have similar difficulties in the work environment!

Your manager and other work contacts (current or past) are obviously an important source of information. Some questions you may want to ask:

- What do you see as my major skills? Strengths?
- What do you see as my major development areas?
- How can I improve how I am seen by others?
- What areas should I try to improve ?
- What kinds of job do you think I can realistically aspire to over the next few years?
- Are you aware of any jobs that I would do well?
- How realistic do you think my career goals are, based on what I've told you?
- What training and/or development do you think I need to attain these goals?
- What are the possible obstacles to me accomplishing my goals?
- What do you see as the key things I could do to improve my chances of achieving my goals?

Remember, people like to be asked for their opinions. Some may surprise you with their candour.

Be prepared to feel a little down when they talk to you about your limitations, and be prepared for the red glow of embarrassment which will come when they start to sing your praises!

If the people you have asked are unused to giving this sort of feedback they may appreciate some notice of your questions. In addition, giving them a copy of the page from the next Activity, 'Selecting a Mentor – Giving Feedback', will help.

Based on the feedback you have received you may wish to develop new skills and abilities. This may be particularly relevant if you're returning to work after a break, e.g., bringing up a family, looking after an elderly relative or full-time education. Some ways of doing this are:

- Working with someone
- Taking a training course
- Continuing your education
- Taking a developmental assignment
- Enlarging your position by taking on responsibilities which will stretch you
- Joining a club or society, especially as a committee member
- Reading

(Clearly some of the options above are only available to people who are currently in work. If you aren't, think laterally to try to identify alternatives, e.g., work placement with a local employer.)

If you were to develop new skills and abilities:

What skills, knowledge or abilities are they?

_____

_____

_____

How will you do this?

_____

_____

_____

In what ways might you want to develop yourself?

_____

_____

_____

How can you do that?

_____

_____

_____

Selecting a mentor

There is no such thing as a 'self-made' man. We are made up of thousands of others. Everyone who has ever done a kind deed for us, or spoken one word of encouragement to us, has entered into the make-up of our character and of our thoughts, as well as our success.

George Matthew Adams

Do you have someone whom you can use as a sounding board for your ideas? As you develop your career, life and jobsearching ideas and plans, you will find it very beneficial to 'bounce' them off someone else. They'll be far more meaningful when you explain them to someone else.

WHO SHOULD YOU ASK?

Ask someone who knows you well and whose opinion you value. You will probably find it best not to use your partner. Please do not misunderstand me – I'm not advising you should exclude your partner; not at all. But they may not be able to 'see the wood for the trees', because of their emotional involvement. If you have access to a professional counsellor you will find it very useful. If not, don't despair. What about a favourite uncle or aunt? An old school/college/university friend? A current or previous work colleague? A neighbour? A fellow member of a sports or social club?

What qualities should a mentor have?

- A mentor should be a – *good listener* – you should do most of the talking.
- A mentor should be *genuine* – someone who has a genuine interest in you.
- There should be mutual *respect* as it is important that you talk as equals.
- A mentor should be *in touch with reality* – if your dreams and goals become unrealistic they should help you back to earth gently.

Remember, your mentor is not your adviser: a good mentor won't begin sentences with 'If I were you I would' … or, 'Why don't you …'. It's your job to develop the ideas and use your mentor as a 'testing ground'.

A simple test to see if they are the right person may be to ask yourself, 'Would I choose them as my boss?'.

WHEN SHOULD YOU MEET?

It is a good idea to have regular meetings for an hour or two weekly or fortnightly.

WHAT ARE THE BENEFITS?

You will find that your plans are modified, refined and more **realistic.** And all it will cost you, is a box of chocolates, a special thank-you at Christmas or a couple of beers!

You may wish to give a photocopy of the next page to your mentor.

SELECTING A MENTOR – GIVING FEEDBACK

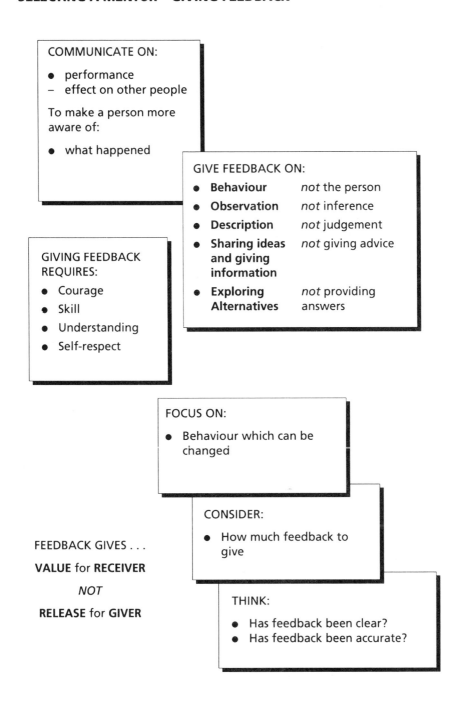

COMMUNICATE ON:

- performance
- effect on other people

To make a person more aware of:

- what happened

GIVE FEEDBACK ON:

- **Behaviour**   *not* the person
- **Observation**   *not* inference
- **Description**   *not* judgement
- **Sharing ideas and giving information**   *not* giving advice
- **Exploring Alternatives**   *not* providing answers

GIVING FEEDBACK REQUIRES:

- Courage
- Skill
- Understanding
- Self-respect

FOCUS ON:

- Behaviour which can be changed

CONSIDER:

- How much feedback to give

FEEDBACK GIVES . . .

VALUE for **RECEIVER**

NOT

RELEASE for **GIVER**

THINK:

- Has feedback been clear?
- Has feedback been accurate?

WHERE AM I GOING?

cutiveAcc
strator Advertising L.
aftEngineer Airline Pilot A.
malTechnicianAnthropologis
okseller Antique Dealer Archaeo.
rchitectArchiver ArtDealer Astron
uctioneer Ballet Dancer Banker Barr
Biochemist Botanist Bookseller Broad
BrokerBuilderCareersAdvisorCart
Cardiologist Chemical Engineer Chii
ClerkCoastguardCommunityWorker
cretaryComputerEngineerConduct
igner Dentist Development Engin
torDispensingOpticianDoctor
ainerDraughtsmanDriving.
istEconomistEditorEducat
calEngineerElectronicEngir
ainer Environmental Heal
iomistEstateAgentE
ortAgentFabricDesig
rmManagerFashionPh
ilmDirectorFinancialMa
ishFarmerFlightControllerF
nologistFootwearManufacture.
OfficeExecutiveForensicScientist.
ForwarderGameKeeperGeneticistG

irdia
rographicSurvey
ormationScientistInsura
teriorDesignerInternational.
velleryDesignerJournalistLand.
awyerLegalAccountantLibrarian
ousekeeperLossAdjusterMagazine
ManagementAccountantMarineEng
'arketingManagerMediaPlannerMe
hysicistMerchantBankerMetallurgi
MicrobiologistMissionaryModelMu
NavalArchitectNeurophysiologistN
ngineerNurseOccupationalThera
ceManagerOpticianPackagin
iterPatentAgentPersonnelM
macistPhysicistPianistPoli
iterProbationOfficerPsychi
blicAdministratorPublis.
reationalManagerR
agerSchoolInspector.
ersonSilversmithSocio
okerSurveyorSystemsAn
TextileDesignerTheatreMai.
gStandardsOfficerTravelAgen
erwriterVeterinarySurgeonWater
outhWorkerZooKeeperZoologistZ

Introduction to Phase II

There is only one success – to be able to spend your life in your way.
CHRISTOPHER MORLEY

Wouldn't it be wonderful if you could work through a few exercises to help you know more about yourself, decide on a new career direction, pick up the newspaper, make a few phone calls and hey presto get a new job.

Life isn't like that and I'm sure you didn't need me to point it out!

So far in this book the principal point of focus has been you. But you don't exist in a vacuum. The job you want is out there in the real world.

We are now going to switch to take a more panoramic view. You will still be a major part of the picture and we will start to summarise some of the things you have learned about yourself in Phase I.

We will also consider the external environment – what jobs could you do? What are good bets for the future and the not so good bets?

I'm not going to offer you a list of jobs though! If I did there wouldn't be space for anything else in the book! Indeed, we would need an extra twenty or thirty volumes.

Through your research activities you will identify job opportunities. Many of which you haven't even thought of so far!

My new direction

A state without the means of some change is without the means of its conservation.

EDMUND BURKE

In this exercise, we will bring together information you have built up about yourself in the earlier activities and put them into the context of the 'outside world' – external environment, so that you can set your course for your new direction.

A technique used widely in business to help in evaluating situations is SLOT analysis. SLOT stands for:

- **S**trengths
- **L**imitations
- **O**pportunities
- **T**hreats

(SLOT – is the American version. British people talk about SWOT analysis where 'W' stands for weakness – I'd rather talk about a person's limitations.)

The SLOT analysis can be an extremely useful technique, for you to think about what you can offer, relative to **your** external environment, i.e., the job market. The SLOT analysis helps you to take stock of your position so that you can plan what you want to do next.

The Strengths and Limitations elements are personal to you. Opportunities and Threats lie in the external environment.

Use the forms on the next pages to build up your own SLOT analysis. It will probably take a few days so do some work on it and keep coming back to it.

Use your SLOT analysis to:

- Identify how you can maximise the use of your strengths.
- See how you can compensate for your limitations.
- Identify opportunities, particularly ones which may not be immediately obvious.
- If at all possible see if threats can be turned into opportunities.

The first part of the exercise (Strengths and Limitations) will be straight-forward, if you have completed the earlier activities. Opportunities and Threats may be more difficult to identify so here are a few examples.

Opportunities: As society changes and technology advances new jobs emerge: 'Conveyancing' shops no longer need a qualified solicitor. Comput-ers need Systems Analysts/Programmers/Operators. Computer networking allows people to work in different locations, e.g. at home. New Prisons are opening with 'contracted' staff. People are becoming more environmentally conscious. 'Fringe' medicine is becoming more acceptable. People are becom-ing more aware of their health and fitness. These are areas where new jobs are emerging.

Threats: These are the external barriers to you achieving your career goals. Like the closure of a major company in your area. Try to see if external threats can be turned into Opportunities. It can sometimes be done. Diane, a friend of mine, wanted to return to her work as a teacher after starting a family. The external 'Threat' to her doing it was that there was no suitable childcare available. If Diane and Keith, her husband, were having difficulty finding nursery places then surely other parents would be having the same problem? Their answer was to start a Day-Care Nursery. Now, in addition to Diane's job as a Teacher and Keith's as a College Lecturer, they jointly run a nursery employing four people.

MY SLOT ANALYSIS

My personal strengths	My personal limitations

MY SLOT ANALYSIS

In my external environment

Opportunities	Threats

EVALUATING YOUR SLOT ANALYSIS

Your SLOT analysis won't provide an instant and magical answer, but, in my experience, very often ideas seem to jump out of the pages when you look at all four factors side by side.

If you are having difficulty coming up with ideas, the next part of this activity will help you.

RESEARCH TIME – JOB IDEAS

If you try to do this part of the activity anywhere other than in your local library, where you have access to directories, careers brochures and a hundred and one sources of valuable information you won't even scratch the surface.

Take yourself off to the library

Take yourself off to the library and ask the librarian to advise on suitable references both in the 'industry and organisations' and the 'careers section'. Alternatively, go to your local Careers Office – they aren't just for school leavers. They're incredibly helpful people and some will start to act as your research assistants, if you explain what you are doing and ask for their advice in the right way!

Don't be in too much of a hurry. Brainstorm ideas with your partner and friends.

Research isn't a 'do it' once and you're finished process either. Keep coming back to this section to add new ideas and to give you inspiration.

JOB IDEAS 1

My ideal job will provide the following: write into the boxes what you would like.

Uses for my Skills and Knowledge	Responsibilities
Working Conditions & Locality	**Salary/Benefits Package**
Interpersonal Environment	**Opportunities**

JOB IDEAS 2

Places where I may be able to find my ideal job: Write down the names of companies, government bodies, charitable organisations, etc. where you may be able to find your ideal job – use library, friends, networking contacts, and yourself as resources.

JOB IDEAS 3

Job names: Write down the names of jobs you could do.

DECISION-MAKING TIME!

When you have invested time and effort in the job ideas exercise, you will arrive at a vast number of options – especially when you combine the different jobs and the different potential workplaces.

If you had an army of secretaries and researchers working for you, then you could allocate tasks and blitz every possibility straight away. The reality of life is that you are probably on your own, so you need to set priorities so that you direct your energies in the right direction.

Now try to prioritise the options available to you so that you arrive at your **top five priority targets**. Your 'Priority Classification Criteria' are the things on the Job Ideas 1 page (also see Activity 8). Very rarely will a job satisfy all of a person's 'ideal' criteria and the same person might identify their five top priority jobs as:

- An Assistant Brand Manager in a large company.
- A Market Research Executive in an Agency
- An Advertising Agency Account Executive
- A Market Research Manager in a large company
- A Brand Manager in a small or medium-sized company

The judge of the importance of each of your 'ideal' factors is **you**. Now write **your** five target positions below:

_____

_____

_____

_____

_____

Targeting

Having identified your priorities you still need to identify your **top priority** so that you can really target **your** jobsearch.

If you make your jobsearch too vague, then you will confuse people in your network, potential employers and recruitment consultants. Which of the above five options is your number one target, or is it difficult to choose?

People use many different decision-making methods. A technique which I have found useful is 'force-field analysis'. Quite simply you write the pros and cons of making a decision alongside each other in lists. When you have collected all of the pros and cons you allocate an arbitrary 'weighting',out of 10, to each point – only you can be the judge. Using force-field analysis takes only a few minutes and can really help in weighing the pros and cons of a decision.

Force-field analysis is a very useful, quick and simple way to evaluate options available to you. It's a more structured way of weighing the pros cons of a situation. Try it!

Active forces	Score	Restraining forces	Score
+ Positives *Why should I go for this option*		− Negatives *What's holding me back?*	
Total +		Total −	

When you evaluate your five options using force-field analysis, the one with the highest score when you have subtracted the 'restraining forces' column from the 'active forces' column is the one you should go for as a first priority.

To give you an example: The force-field analysis is the one I used to help me to decide whether or not to start my own business.

FORCE-FIELD ANALYSIS EXAMPLE:

Active forces	Score	Restraining forces	Score
+ Positives *Why should I go for this option*		− Negatives *What's holding me back?*	
Master of my own destiny	10	Lack of predictable income	6
Earnings potential	7	Long-term security	5
Variety	7	Away from home?	5
Government aid/advice	5	Lack of permanence	3
Redundancy package available	8	Need office	2
I can set company's direction	8	Health insurance/life assurance	2
I am able to work alone	7	Pension	3
Market exists	7	Lack of challenge from peers	5
Resources (me + support)	9	Collection of revenue	5
		Ability to obtain mortgage	5
		Not seeing job through	5
		No income	2
Total +	68	Total −	48

Even though there were **more negative reasons** than positive ones, the **'strength' of the positive argument won!**

PRIORITY 1 TARGET

Evaluate your options using the force-field analysis format below.

Aim for your number one target.

As you start to exhaust the possibilities for your number one target move to number two, etc.

Targeting your jobsearch gives you a clear direction to move in, just like having a well-printed map.

Active forces	Score	Restraining forces	Score
+ Positives *Why should I go for this option*		− Negatives *What's holding me back?*	
Total +		Total −	

Networking – contact development

Putting off an easy thing makes it hard and putting off a hard one makes it impossible.

GEORGE H. LONMER

A new word has crept into the English language in the past few years: 'Networking' or contact development. For many, it's something they have been doing for years quite naturally. For others the thought of it makes them feel so uncomfortable that it makes the hairs on the back of their neck stand up.

I talk about networking in Activity 27 'The Way In – Finding Vacant Jobs' and in other parts of the book. However, I believe that networking is so important to you in your jobsearch that it deserves a separate mention. Networking is the proactive process of maximising the relationships you already have and using these contacts to help you to identify work opportunities. Why is networking important? Some people believe that as few as 25 per cent of jobs are ever advertised. But someone must know about the rest! Also, career consultants will tell you that networking becomes increasingly important as you get older. About 50 per cent of people over 40 find a job through personal contacts.

Networking is not about pestering people for a job to the point that none of your friends will ever speak to you. Nor is it about embarrassing people so that they feel morally obliged to help you or even give you a job.

Networking is about approaching people genuinely to ask for advice and ideas on how you can get your next job: You aren't meeting them, telephoning or writing to them for a job. This is extremely important. When you make it quite clear that what you want from them is advice and ideas, you'll reduce their embarrassment about the contact and you will find them far more forthcoming.

Enough of their embarrassment! Broadcasting that you're on the dole (if you are), is a real ego booster for you isn't it?! I think not. So how are you going to say it? Some people find it very difficult to tell others that they are looking for work, so if we can overcome this barrier quickly you will be able to start networking straight away. Look at the following expressions.

Words used to describe what has happened to an organisation

Restructured	Gone bankrupt	We merged with another company
Contracted	Called in the receivers	My face didn't fit any longer
Downsized	The banks foreclosed	We had a change of management
Reorganised	We were taken over	We had a de-merger

Words used to describe the effects it has on people:

Fired	Organised out	Dismissed	Booted out
Sacked	Let go	Axed	Dropped
Given P45	Said good-bye	Bounced	Let out
Made redundant	Surplus	Discharged	Terminated

In the space below write down why you are looking for work. Don't be self-effacing and don't be critical of your (previous) employer.

_____

_____

_____

_____

Now say it four or five times out loud.

The 'bottom line' is still the same, but you should now feel a lot more comfortable in explaining to people why you're looking for work and why you're asking for their help and advice.

WHO SHOULD I CONTACT

Many people think they have only a small network, of personal contacts until they do this exercise. Go through your address book, diary, business card file, customer records, correspondence files, etc., and brainstorm. Write down the names of people whom you know in the appropriate spaces on the next two pages.

When you have completed these two pages, they will be some of the most valuable pages in this book.

At this point **include anyone and everyone you can think of.** Ask your partner and close friends for ideas. **You have started networking!**

MY NETWORK

Bankers	Competitors

Customers	Club members

Consultants	Doctors/Dentist/Solicitor

Friends

MY NETWORK (continued)

Neighbours	Professional contacts
Suppliers	**University/College/School colleagues**
Past employers	**Relatives**
Teachers	**Work colleagues**

NOW I'VE GOT MY NETWORK – WHAT NEXT?

We need to identify whom you should contact first. So who are the best people to contact from **your** network?

- People whom you can contact relatively easily.
- Aim high – the higher up the organisation the better.
- People who could potentially employ you are even better.
- People on the same level, but different function who can 'pass you on' to their peer. (People on the same level with the same function may see you as a competitor.) People on a lower level are rarely useful except for information gathering.

Now **choose the top fifteen names** on your list and contact them. Decide whether you should go to see them in person, write or telephone.

Whatever you do, get to the point quickly, don't waste their time. Achieve your three objectives:

1. To **let them know you are looking for work** – so that they can keep their eyes and ears open.
2. To **ask them for the names of two of their contacts** whom you might approach.
3. To **ask for their advice** about opportunities/recruitment consultants/journals/ads they might have seen.

Remember, you get one opportunity to make a first impression. The most powerful 'in' you can get is a personal introduction. As people give you the names of people in their network do what you can to make a positive first impression.

Don't over-stretch yourself by using the blunderbuss technique. If you try to contact everyone in your network on day one you won't be able to handle the workload. Keep prioritising and manage the project, e.g., following-up with a phone call if you've said you will.

Whenever you have made contact with one of your network, either in person, or by telephone send a short 'thank-you' letter. It costs little and shows your genuine appreciation.

Happy networking!

Goal setting

When I was young I observed that nine out of every ten things I did were failures, so I did ten times more work.

GEORGE BERNARD SHAW

'*A Goal is a dream taken seriously*', or put another way – from 'SOUTH PACIFIC': '*You've got to have a dream, if you don't have a dream, How are you going to have a dream come true?*' In this activity we will formalise your dreams about the future into goals.

WHY IS GOAL SETTING IMPORTANT?

Goal setting gives you a target to aim for. Organisations and businesses constantly use goal setting to help them to achieve things like production and sales targets. Similarly, many successful people say that an element of their success is due to goal setting. Goals are specific: 'to be happy' is not a goal. It is an aim. Achieving goals is the process of putting one foot after the next, along the stepping stones, which lead to happiness. A good test of a goal is to see if it is **SMART**.

Specific – e.g., if it is to get a job, list the title, type of organisation, etc.
Measurable – what criteria will you use to measure your achievement?
Achievable – You will become demotivated if you fail to achieve your goal – but don't make it too easy, make it challenging.
Relevant – goals should directly relate to what you want to achieve.
Timed – set a target completion date.
An example of a jobsearcher's goals could be:
Each day next week I will make contact with a minimum of three people on my network list and will get two more names from each of them.'
A longer-term goal might be:
'Within four months I will get a job as a Development Engineer, in a medium/large electronics company, within 30 miles of home, on £X,000 per year.'
I know they sound a bit wordy but 'I'm going to make some phone calls and I'm going to get a job in electronics', just aren't goals. Goals state what you need to do to reach your aims.

Goals can be short or long term and relate to all aspects of life.

Use the form on the next page to help **you** to **set your goals**. Set the long-term goals first, then your short-term goals.

GOAL SETTING

I am going to achieve the following career and life goals in the next five years.

Goals	Home & Family	Work	Social & Community	Self (leisure, study, etc.)
Long term: 6 months				
1 year				
2 years				
5 years				
Short term: Today				
1 week				
1 month				

Make a note below of what you might need to do to resolve any conflicts:

_____

_____

_____

_____

☺ My Jobsearching Do's ☺

_____

_____

_____

_____

☹ My Jobsearching Don'ts ☹

_____

_____

_____

_____

Use these notepads to summarise your learning points as you complete activities in *I Can Do That!*

Managing my jobsearching project

Lost yesterday, somewhere between sunrise and sunset, two golden hours, each set with sixty diamond minutes. No reward is offered, they are gone forever.

Horace Mann

If you're currently working and also jobsearching then you have a challenging job balancing your time between the two. If your current full-time occupation is jobsearching then the apparent lack of structure can be daunting in that it can scare some people into doing anything; that bit of decorating I've been putting off, or a visit to long lost friends – anything other than jobsearching. The answer to both is to have planning and control systems.

ORGANISE YOURSELF AND MANAGE YOUR TIME

Jobsearching is a job.

- Allocate some 'office space' at home where you can work undisturbed.
- Keep a diary and use it both for planning your time and recording appointments.
- Have a 'filing system', either using files, box files or ring binders.
- Work expands to fill the time available – set deadlines for each task.
- Set daily objectives; use the daily action planner on page 91 and stick to it.
- Prioritise the day's tasks A: Must; B: should; C: could. Only move to the Bs when the As are finished, and to the Cs when the Bs are finished. Don't do the Cs first just because they can be done quickly. Subdivide As into A1, A2, A3, and **do A1 now!**
- Block off times in your diary for different parts of your jobsearch.
- Decide when you are at your best for doing things, e.g., best at telephoning early morning, good at planning early evening.
- Plan for tomorrow at the end of today.
- Start each day by making progress against an A1.

- After you have opened and sorted your mail, handle each piece of paper only once – in other words, only pick up a piece of paper from your 'in' tray when you intend to do something with it.
- Accumulate non-essential reading together and scan it for 20 minutes each week.
- Add additional actions to your personal action plan as they arise throughout the day and prioritise them.
- Each week complete the Weekly Jobsearch Report (see below), as an evaluation of how you are progressing against achieving your goals.

PROCRASTINATION IS THE THIEF OF TIME. DO IT NOW!

Don't be like a colleague of my friend Ann, who bought a motivational cassette tape on procrastination, but never got round to listening to it!

JOBSEARCH PERFORMANCE AND PLANNING SUMMARY

Week ending (Day/Date:)

THIS WEEK	GOALS FOR NEXT WEEK
I wrote _____ jobsearch letters.	I will complete _____ applications.
I sent ____ resumes and ____letters to potential employers.	I will make _____jobsearch telephone calls.
I completed _____ applications.	I will complete _____ hours of job research.
I made _____ jobsearch telephone calls.	I will set up _____ appointments for networking interviews.
I completed _____ hours of job research.	I will conduct ____ networking interviews
I set up _____ appointments for network interviews.	I will follow up on _____contacts and ___ referrals.
I conducted _____ networking interviews.	
I received _____ invitiations to a job interview.	
I followed up on _ contacts and ___ referrals.	

(Copyright waiver – this form may be photocopied for personal use of purchasers.)

PERSONAL ACTION PLAN

Your Name:		Date:	
Today's Goals:			

Action Plan:	A/B/C	Deadline	Completed

Carry forward uncompleted tasks to tomorrow:

Working for myself

Diligence is the mother of good luck
BENJAMIN FRANKLIN

HEALTH & WEALTH WARNING

DON'T DO IT!

Have I put you off? The chances are that your earnings will be lower than you anticipate. Your working hours will be longer than you have ever worked before and you will stretch your personal relationships to their limits, or maybe even beyond.

It may be that as you have worked through the activities in this book you have started to think that you would like to become self-employed. If my Health & Wealth warning has put you off then I've done you a great favour! You'll appreciate the scope of this book is to advise people on how to gain paid employment.

If you're considering self-employment gather as much information as you can. I have included sources of useful information in the Appendix. The Department of Employment has an excellent 'Induction scheme' (details from your Job Centre) for new business start-ups. The High Street banks produce free information packs (the NatWest one is very useful.)

Talk to as many people as you can, who run their own businesses: your friendly fish & chip shop owner; local landlord, newsagent, etc. No matter what the business, the potential problems are usually the same – cash flow, marketing, obtaining supplies. With the greatest of respect to college lecturers and counsellors, it will only be from talking to self-employed people, that you'll find out what it's really like. You'll also hear, no doubt, of the enormous satisfaction that comes from being self-employed. But I don't want to over-sell.

Most importantly of all, **talk** your idea through with your partner. His/her support is essential.

If, when you have gathered all of the information, you are totally committed to it, abandon your jobsearch. You cannot do either of them half-heartedly and ... Go For It!

Good luck. You'll need it.

HOW WILL I GET THERE?

...utive/Acc.
.strator Advertising.
aftEngineerAirlinePilotA.
.malTechnicianAnthropologis
ooksellerAntiqueDealerArchaeo.
.rchitectArchiverArtDealerAstron
.uctioneerBalletDancerBankerBarr
BiochemistBotanistBooksellerBroad
BrokerBuilderCareersAdvisorCart'
CardiologistChemicalEngineerChir
ClerkCoastguardCommunityWorker
.cretaryComputerEngineerConduct
.ignerDentistDevelopmentEngin
.torDispensingOpticianDoctor
.rainerDraughtsmanDriving.
.istEconomistEditorEducat
.calEngineerElectronicEngir
.ainerEnvironmentalH
.iomistEstateAgentE
.ortAgentFabricDesig
.rmManagerFashionPh
.rilmDirectorFinancialMa.
.ishFarmerFlightControllerF
.nologistFootwearManufacture.
OfficeExecutiveForensicScientist.
ForwarderGameKeeperGeneticistG

.rographicSurvey.
.ormationScientistInsura.
.teriorDesignerInternational.
.velleryDesignerJournalistLand.
.awyerLegalAccountantLibrarian
ousekeeperLossAdjusterMagazine
ManagementAccountantMarineEng
'arketingManagerMediaPlannerM.
.nysicistMerchantBankerMetallurgi
MicrobiologistMissionaryModelMu'
NavalArchitectNeurophysiologistN
.ngineerNurseOccupationalThera'
.ceManagerOpticianPackagin.
.terPatentAgentPersonnelM
.macistPhysicistPianistPoli
.terProbationOfficerPsychia
.ublicAdministratorPublis.
.reationalManagerR.
.agerSchoolInspector.
.ersonSilversmithSocio
.okerSurveyorSystemsAi.
TextileDesignerTheatreMar.
.gStandardsOfficerTravelAgen
.erwriterVeterinarySurgeonWater
.uthWorkerZooKeeperZoologistZ

Introduction to Phase II

The three great essentials to achieve anything worthwhile are first, hard work; second, stick-to-itiveness; third, common sense

Thomas A. Eddison

What we have done so far has been to develop your strategic direction. This section is devoted to the tactics of getting a job.

Think of each of the activities as a different skill of a craftsperson – **you**. The activities are the tools to help you to get your new job.

Work on those activities which will help **you** to develop those skills, which **you** need to help you to get the job you want.

Using the telephone to my advantage

Speak clearly, if you speak at all;
carve every word before you let it fall.

OLIVER WEDNELL HOLMES

Used effectively the telephone can get you past security guards, along hallowed corridors and into the office of decision makers!

Whether you are telephoning to confirm an appointment for an interview or at the start of your jobsearch, you will find the following tips, which are taught to telesales people, helpful.

- Make sure you have a pen and paper ready along with any relevant documents.

- Smile – I know it feels silly when you're the only one in the room, but it adds sparkle to your voice.

- Stand up! All of your internal viscera are pushing up against your diaphragm and squeezing the confidence out of your voice. Standing up makes you more assertive and makes you sound more convincing!

- Have a clear objective of what you want to achieve, along with a fall-back, e.g., primary objective to arrange an informal meeting; secondary objective to call back tomorrow, when they have had a chance to read your résumé, to arrange a meeting.

- Make sure your language is convincing, fluent and understandable.

- Prepare your script in advance – write down your agenda.

- Practise your script, e.g., the direct approach:

  Hello Mr. _____. Ms. _____. I'm _____. You recently received a copy of my résumé. I'm calling to see if we can make an appointment to meet informally to discuss any vacancies you might have for Management Accountants?'

- Have your diary ready!

- Keep a written record of every conversation.

OVERCOMING DEFENCES

The higher up the organisation you go then the higher and wider the barriers seem to become with receptionists and secretaries seemingly having no other purpose than to protect their bosses!

The higher up the organisation you go ...

The following techniques range from the polite to the devious. All of them work!

- Find out the secretary's name from the receptionist. Address him/her personally and repeat the name at least twice when requesting to be put through.

- When you're networking and you're put through to a secretary say it's 'a personal call' – (most managers will take 'personal calls' since most of them think it's a call from a head-hunter!). Get to the point quickly. If it's a friend of a friend, make sure you clarify it straight away.

- Beat the system by calling the manager at around 8.00 am or after 6.00 pm (i.e., before or after work for most secretaries) or when the secretary is at lunch.

- If you try phoning most companies during normal working hours and ask for the name of the Marketing Director, almost invariably the receptionists will tell you politely, but firmly, that they are not allowed to give that information over the telephone.

- Ring at around 8.30 pm and you're likely to speak to a lonely security guard, who is looking after the telephones, along with the odd million pounds worth of building! Speak to them politely and explain that you want to call the Marketing Director the next day and you just wanted to make sure you'd got the right offices. They'll be glad of someone to talk to and will probably reel off a list of names and extension numbers – if you ask for them, have your pen ready.

- Use a 'third-party recommendation' like 'Mr Robinson, your Personnel Manager has asked me to get in touch with ...'

Remember, you may need to kiss a lot of frogs before you can find a prince! But persistence does pay!

Activity 20

Letter writing

A law of nature rules that energy cannot be destroyed. You change its form from coal to steam, from steam to power in the turbine, but you do not destroy energy. In the same way, another law governs human activity and rules that honest effort cannot be lost, but that some day the proper benefits will be forthcoming.

PAUL SPEICHER

If you can see someone in person do it. If you can't see them personally, speak to them on the telephone. If you can't speak to them on the telephone, write a letter.

Realistically, you will have to write a lot of letters. Learn from the people in direct-marketing who write letters to customers for a living. Why? Because through your letters you are trying to sell another person the idea that 'they should meet you', that 'they should look at your CV', etc. When it comes down to it, it's a sales letter.

AIDA is the Copywriter's greatest friend. If you look at well-written 'direct mail' letters they follow the AIDA format:

A   **Attention** – The first paragraph quickly comes to the point to grab the reader's attention.

I   **Interest** – The second gives information to arouse the reader's interest.

D   **Desire** – The third paragraph talks about the benefits you will gain and what it will be like for you to own the product or service.

A   **Action** – Now you want the product or service what do you do? Telephone, fill a form etc.?

Sounds simple doesn't it? Would that it were that straightforward!

As you write letters of application, letters to networking contacts, letters to request application forms, covering letters to go with your CV, or letters to recruitment consultants, check to see if they follow the AIDA principles.

Try to see the letter from the recipient's viewpoint. What impression would it make on you? What would you do when you received it?

The following pages contain some general tips on letter writing which many people, who are unused to letter writing, find useful.

LETTER WRITING – USEFUL TIPS

- Use quality paper. A4, ideally, with a printed address (from your High Street print-shop. Don't ask for the address to be printed in blue – it doesn't photocopy too well).
- Handwriting is OK if it's legible. A word-processed letter is almost always OK, unless you have been specifically asked to submit a hand-written application.
- There should be no spelling mistakes, grammatical errors or scruffy lay-out. But that can't happen! Don't you believe it! When I recruited a secretary recently I rejected over half of the applications for these reasons. The advertisement asked for 'accuracy'!
- Write to a named person wherever you can.
- 'Dear Mr' is straightforward for men. If you don't know whether a woman is a 'Mrs' or 'Miss' then 'Ms' is the safest bet these days. These letters end 'Yours sincerely' (small 's').
- When you have to write 'Dear Sir' or 'Dear Madam' (note no 'e' at the end), then these letters end 'Yours faithfully' (small 'f').
- If an advertisement asks you to apply to Peter Butler do not start letter 'Dear Peter' – it's over-familiar unless you know Peter personally. Even then be cautious, since your letter may be photocopied and circulated to other people.
- Be succinct – get to the point quickly. If your letter is more than one page long, then edit it.
- Match the skills and knowledge that you have to the ones the recruiter is looking for, i.e., those mentioned either in the job description or the advertisement.
- Never, never, never be self-effacing – 'I'm not quite what you're looking for but I'll give it a go anyway!' And don't point out anything which is missing from your portfolio of skills and knowledge that they are looking for! It's their job to spot that!

On the following pages I have included some sample letters. They are not offered as definitive examples, but hopefully they will provide the spark of inspiration you need if you are sitting staring out of the window with a blank sheet of paper in front of you!

Letter to request an application form

4 Stable Cottages
Abthorpe
Northamptonshire
NN12 8QT
Tel 123 7777777

23 March 1994

Mr G Choice
Moderate Corporation
Science Park
Daventry Road
Northants
NN99 99NN

Dear Mr Choice

RE: CE/23393

I noticed your advertisement in the Chronicle & Echo newspaper for a Laboratory Supervisor. I would be very grateful if you will send me an application form.

I look forward to hearing from you.

Yours sincerely

Janet Dickson (Mrs)

NOTE
● Don't enclose a CV or anything else at this point. Follow their system.

Covering letter with CV

4 Stable Cottages
Abthorpe
Northamptonshire
NN12 8QT
Tel 123 7777777

23 March 1994

Mr G Choice
Moderate Corporation
Science Park
Daventry Road
Northants
NN99 99NN

Dear Mr Choice

I would like to apply for the post of Accounts Supervisor which was advertised recently in the Chronicle & Echo.

I have read the job description with great interest and enclose my completed application form.

I look forward to hearing from you.

Yours sincerely

Janet Dickson (Mrs)

NOTE
● Don't antagonise them by implying that you're bound to get an interview. If you are too presumptuous you'll turn them off.
● This letter does very little, however, to help the recruiter to match the candidate to the job. It would have been a good idea to include three or four features, advantages, or benefit statements (see Activity 23 'Selling Myself')

Response to an advertised vacancy

4 Stable Cottages
Abthorpe
Northamptonshire
NN12 8QT
Tel 123 7777777

23 March 1994

Mr G Choice
Moderate Corporation
Science Park
Daventry Road
Northants
NN99 99NN

Dear Mr Choice

Ref: MCC/737 – Production Manager: Chronicle & Echo 22.3.94

I am writing in response to the above advertisement and wish to apply for the position.

You will see from my CV that for the past five years, I have managed a plant manufacturing shampoos and hair colourants on a continuous production basis. Many of the production features appear to be very similar to your own. Previously I worked as Materials Planning Manager in a high-volume batch production plant.

I believe I have all of the qualities you have outlined in your advertisement – BS5750 trained, a strong leader and capacity for hard work.

I am now seeking an appointment where my experience can be fully utilised.

I look forward to hearing from you.

Yours sincerely

Janet Dickson (Mrs)

NOTE

- This letter highlights what the candidate has to offer against the recruiter's requirements, but isn't a 're-write' of the CV.

A speculative letter to a targeted potential employer

4 Stable Cottages
Abthorpe
Northamptonshire
NN12 8QT
Tel 123 7777777

23 March 1994

Mr G Choice
Moderate Corporation
Science Park
Daventry Road
Northants
NN99 99NN

Dear Mr Choice

Ref: An Opportunity to Increase Your Market Share and Reduce Operating Costs

As the Marketing Director (Electronic Products) of a £50m turnover UK company, I have initiated and managed improvement programmes that have reversed sales and profit declines.

Some of my achievements include:
- launching 6 new products over the last two years and increasing market share substantially.
- increasing sales by 12% by exploiting new markets.
- reducing marketing operation overheads by £125,000 by introducing effective controls.
- introducing networked computer-based information and financial control systems to improve customer response times and invoicing
- sales and profit forecasting on a monthly basis with 90% + accuracy.

My CV is enclosed as I am now actively looking for a new position. I would be very glad to give you more information or to come and see you.

Yours sincerely

Janet Dickson (Mrs)

Enc.

NOTE
● Four or five achievement statements should be just right. You want to stimulate their interest and leave them wanting to know more.

Making something out of nothing

4 Stable Cottages
Abthorpe
Northamptonshire
NN12 8QT
Tel 123 7777777

23 March 1994

Mr G Choice
Moderate Corporation
Science Park
Daventry Road
Northants
NN99 99NN

Dear Mr Choice

It was kind of you to read my CV and write to me on 19th March.

I was disappointed to learn that there are no openings in your company. It would have been a fortunate coincidence if my letter had reached you when you were recruiting for someone with my background.

May I ask you whether you can suggest the names of any other people whom I might contact?

I know that managers like yourself are often asked by others to 'keep their eyes open' for people with my skills and knowledge. I would very much appreciate you referring me to any of your acquaintances who could be interested. I shall welcome any additional suggestions that you can give.

Many thanks in anticipation

Yours sincerely

Janet Dickson (Mrs)

NOTE

● What have you got to lose? This letter is also worth trying with recruitment consultants – they may refer you to a 'competitor'

Speculative letter to a recruitment consultant

4 Stable Cottages
Abthorpe
Northamptonshire
NN12 8QT
Tel 123 7777777

23 March 1994

Ms H Hunter
Choose Well Consultants
Northampton Road
Wappenham
Northants
NN99 9NN

Dear Ms Hunter

I am seeking a new appointment where my general management experience in the hotel and catering industry can be used. Any dynamic and developing business area which involves direct customer contact would particularly interest me. I am also keen to continue to develop my general management skills.

My present company is undergoing a period of substantial change and so I believe this an ideal opportunity to review my career to date and investigate other possibilities.

I am willing to relocate within Europe. My current remuneration package includes: a basic salary of £25,000 per annum, a 10% (variable) bonus, fully expensed car, private healthcare and a non-contributory pension scheme.

I enclose my CV and will be glad of any advice you can provide.

Yours sincerely

Janet Dickson (Mrs)

NOTE
- Note that salary package details are included in approaches to recruitment consultants so that they can match you against vacancies. Also, different consultants often deal with jobs at different levels.

Follow-up thank you letter after networking

4 Stable Cottages
Abthorpe
Northamptonshire
NN12 8QT
Tel 123 7777777

23 March 1994

Mr G Choice
Moderate Corporation
Science Park
Daventry Road
Northants
NN99 99NN

Dear Mr Choice

Many thanks for meeting with me last week. I really did appreciate the comments you made about the way I have embarked on my jobsearch.

Thank you also for putting me in contact with Simon and Pat. I have arranged to meet Pat next week, but Simon seems to spend all of his time in meetings – I'll keep trying!

I'll let you know how I get on.

Kind regards.

Yours sincerely

Janet Dickinson

NOTE
- This letter is far less formal than any of the others, but is still business-like.
- If you promise a friend that you'll let them know how you got on, then do it – they want to know and in a couple of weeks they may have some new information for you!

Writing my CV

When I see a bird that walks like a duck and swims like a duck, I call that bird a duck.

RICHARD CARDINAL CUSHING

Imagine yourself in your smartest clothes, looking as well-groomed as you have ever looked in your life and carrying that facial expression of quiet (but not arrogant) confidence.

Your CV (Curriculum Vitae), or résumé, or as some call it 'personal and career history', is a written equivalent to the mental picture you have just formed.

In almost all of the contacts you make, whether networking, speculative applications or responses to advertisements, your CV and introductory letter **will** make the difference to whether or not you get an interview.

The decision between a '**regret**' (sorry you've missed your chance), a '**regret, but hold**' (you're not exactly what we're looking for at present but we'll keep your details on file) and an '**invite for interview'** can be made in as little as 30 seconds!'

If you think this is unrealistic then pity Geoff, a colleague of mine who advertised two jobs in a car assembly plant and got 1,400 replies! Two hundred responses to an advertisement is not at all uncommon.

You need to help the recruiter positively to 'screen you in'. The job of your CV is to take you through the paper 'screening process' to an inteview.

RECRUITERS ARE ALL DIFFERENT

There is an expression that goes: 'If you are ill and ask three Harley Street specialists for a second opinion then you'll get five different opinions!' In the same way recruiters have personal preferences in how they like to see CVs written. For these reasons it is not advisable to be dogmatic. Added to which, your CV is a very personal document – in the final analysis you are the best judge of whether your CV best represents you.

On page 112 is a 'CV Summary' which will help you to gather the relevant information and some example CVs that will help you to decide on which layout you like best can be found on pages 115–124.

BASIC PRINCIPLES

- Use clean laser-printed originals, with a legible font:

  This is in 8 point Times New Roman PS.

  `This is in 10 point New Courier.`

  This is in 12 point Helvetica.

- Use quality paper

- Be brief – use one or two pages if possible. You can do it! Screening of CVs is brief. If the most relevant item is on page 7 paragraph 6 forget it!

- Beware of jargon! Write in plain English if you're a Logistics Manager, a Military Officer, a Research Scientist, etc. Indeed, if you are a specialist of any kind, you will almost certainly have your own vocabulary. Use plain English!

- Be specific – *'I have five years experience in ...'* says far more than *'I have wide experience of ...'*, as does *'I reduced inventory from £4.2m to £1.8m in a period of 12 months'* compared with *'We made substantial savings by reducing our inventory'*

- Get a professional typist to word-process your CV for you. A dot-matrix printer or daisywheel typewriter is just not good enough. Invest in getting someone to do it for you. Local newspapers and newsagents' windows are a good source. Ask to see previous examples and make sure they keep a copy for future updating and so that you can 'personalise' key strengths to produce a targeted CV to fit each job.

- Proof-read, proof-read, proof-read. Start at the bottom of the page and read backwards. You may thimk there are no mistakes, but by reading backwards you see each word in isolation and can spot errors and mis-spellings. For example did you spot <u>thimk</u> in the last sentence or did you read what you thought was there?

- Some recruiters like a margin on the left-hand side so that they can make notes.

- Since CVs are often separated from letters of application so ensure that your name and address are there clearly and write your name at the top of each page – it will help if pages become detached and it will also help an interviewer to remember your name when they are halfway through an interview!

- Presentation 'gimmicks' – personally I like to receive CVs from people who have had them bound or who have attached a photograph. It says that they are prepared to put that bit of extra effort into their application. I know, however, that many of my fellow Human Resources Professionals would strongly disagree. Your decision has to be based on the job and what you know about the organisation.

- If you're applying for your first job or are returning to work after bringing up a family, help the recruiter to recognise your transferable skills

President of the Outdoor Pursuits Society and qualified Mountain Leader implies leadership and someone trained to cope with adversity. Treasurer of the Parish Church Council implies financial skills and abilities to deal with contractors, etc.; spell it out for them.

THE LANGUAGE OF CVs

'It ain't what you say, it's the way that you say it'. This is not totally true' but there is an element of truth to it! Striking a balance between being positive and sounding arrogant can be a real challenge.

Use active words **not** passive words: '**I was responsible for managing** a Project Team which installed a new mainframe computer' is far more powerful than '**I was involved in** installing a new mainframe computer'. The first statement is far more powerful, while the second statement might mean no more than you plugged it in and switched it on!

Passive words that you should avoid are: *liaised with, co-ordinated* and *administered*. The following action verbs will be useful for helping you to write your CV and for letters of application.

ACTION VERBS

accelerated	extended	reduced	terminated
accomplished	finished	reorganised	traced
achieved	generated	revised	traded
approved	implemented	scheduled	trained
conceived	improved	serviced	transferred
conducted	increased	simplified	translated
completed	introduced	set up	tripled
consolidated	launched	sold	trimmed
created	maintained	solved	turned
decided	negotiated	started	uncovered
delivered	ordered	structured	united
developed	performed	streamlined	utilised
demonstrated	pioneered	strengthened	vacated
designed	planned	stressed	waged
directed	processed	stretched	widened
doubled	programmed	succeeded	won
eliminated	proposed	summarised	worked
ended	promoted	superseded	wrote
established	purchased	supervised	
expanded	redesigned		

But beware; don't overdo it. The recruiter is looking for a mortal!

Try reading your finished version to your partner or close friend. If you go a little pink you're probably spot on – bright red and you've overdone it!

How to avoid the convoluted and imprecise expressions and words used by applicants – 'Brevity is best'

AVOID	USE
As a result of this project the company's costs were cut by …	This cut costs by …
During the period referred to in the previous sentence …	I …
As a consequence of the success of this project I was asked to take up the more senior appointment of …	I was promoted …
In this position I …	I …
Considerable elements of my responsibilities were …	I was responsible for …
anticipate	expect
behind schedule	late
prior to	before
personnel	people
proceeded to	then
inaugurated	set up
initiated	started
terminated	ended

CV CHECKLIST

This checklist combines the should (**in bold**) and could (in *italic*) be included items. Use this in combination with the CV Summary on the following pages to help you to gather information and to develop your own CV.

- **Name, address and telephone number(s) stating daytime contact.**
- *Marital Status* (some people prefer to exclude this).
- *Number of dependants and ages* (some people prefer to exclude this).
- *Nationality.*
- *Date of birth / age.*
- **School, College/University attended normally only from age of 11 onwards.**
- **Qualifications: for a recent graduate looking for a first job state 'O' and 'A' Level subjects and pass level, along with subjects taken and class of degree. Or a 45 year old Divisional Director 6 'O' Levels, 3 'A' Levels, BSc 2(i) Chemistry is usually sufficient, although for some**

professions, e.g., Accountancy, you may still wish to include 'A' Level grades.

- *Language proficiency.*
- *Willingness to relocate* (omit if you aren't), *especially if you're out of commuting distance.*
- **Current/last job first, then work backwards through your career, allocating most space to recent job(s) with brief mentions of your early career. Give a one or two sentence summary of the company products/services and their annual turnover, summarise your responsibilities and achievements against each job.**
- *Current/last salary and benefits package, e.g., company car. Be brief. (Opinions differ on whether salary should be included – you may wish to keep your cards close to your chest and risk missing an opportunity because they think you'll be 'too expensive'.)*
- *Career aims.*
- *Personal strengths.*
- *Leisure activities. Be realistic; a one-week skiing holiday five years ago does not qualify you as a skier! Include a variety to show that you have broad interests, but not too many – they may think you'll have no time left for work! Three to four activities are adequate.*
- *Professional achievements, e.g., titles of research papers or articles you have had published. But don't, like someone who once sent me a twenty-seven page CV, append the papers!*
- *Memberships of professional institutions and whether by examination or election.*
- *Do not include referees, unless you're applying for a job in the public sector.*
- *Driving licence – clean and current don't mean the same!*

You need to help the reader positively to 'screen you in'

CV SUMMARY

Name:	**Address:**	**Tel:**

Strengths: *four or five **short** sentences of **your** personal strengths. A four or five sentence summary of your career; who you are and what you have to offer. Make every word count!*

Education and Qualifications: *Right here up front if you have a First-class Honours Degree, PhD and MBA. You may wish to leave to the end if your business achievements outshine your academic ones!*

Career History: *Most recent first and work backwards. Include responsibilities and quantified achievements. Reduce the information as you go back, e.g., five achievements for your current/most recent job. One from a job fifteen years ago.*

Professional Memberships etc:

Personal Information: Willingness to relocate, marital status, etc.

EXAMPLES OF RÉSUMÉS/CVs

The following pages of CVs will be useful in helping you to write your own CV.

I have included my own one-page résumé, which I use to send to clients and publishers, as an example of what can be squeezed into one page.

The other CVs are those of people who have been kind enough to offer them as examples. All have been disguised to 'protect' the individuals and companies concerned.

None of the examples is offered as a definitive example. All of them are unique to the people who wrote them. I hope that from each you will be able to take learning points to enable you to develop your own **unique, personal and effective CV**. Use the table below to help you.

Note: The CVs on the following pages have been printed on both sides of the page. Your CV should be single-sided to make it easier for employers to photocopy.

LEARNING POINTS FROM OTHER PEOPLE'S CVs

Things I like – to use in my own CV	Things I don't like – to avoid in my own CV

Malcolm Hornby

Résumé

Malcolm Hornby is Director of Delta Management, a consultancy which specialises in helping people to develop their teamwork, leadership and communication skills.

His previous experience includes:

Company Personnel Manager: Bristol-Myers Co. Ltd.

Managing the group's Personnel Department, providing a full personnel service to Bristol-Myers Pharmaceutical, Consumer and Clairol Companies on manufacturing, distribution and Head Office sites.

Company Training Manager: Bristol-Myers Co. Ltd.

Having company-wide responsibility for training and development at all levels.

Head of Sales Training: Eli Lilly & Co. Ltd.

Responsible for initial training and ongoing training of the sales force.

Other positions within Eli Lilly were:

Hospital Sales Manager – Managing a sales force selling pharmaceuticals to hospitals in the South of England.

Marketing Associate – responsible for market research and for developing sales and marketing plans.

Pharmaceutical Representative – selling pharmaceuticals to GPs, hospital doctors and pharmacists.

Previously Malcolm taught chemistry and biology in Liverpool and in Paupa New Guinea with Voluntary Service Overseas.

He is tutor with the Open University's Business School, teaching Human Resource Strategies to MBA students, has published numerous articles on communication skills* and is the author of '*I Can Do That*!'.

Malcolm is a Fellow of the Institute of Personnel and Development, Chair of his local branch and a member of the National Council.

Contact Delta Management: 0327 857374

---

* Published in: The Institute of Training and Development Journal, Graduate Careers, Mind Your Own Business, Practice Management, The Journal of the The Institute of Management Specialists, Managing Schools Today.

STEVEN JOHNSON

22 Coventry Road, Egbaston,
Birmingham B66 77BM

HOME TEL: (0303) 30303

Highly motivated, energetic 44 year old Senior Manager having successfully achieved objectives through developing people. A natural leader with strong interpersonal and communication skills who thrives on being involved in leading teams in an environment of creativity and constant challenge. Responsible for results of a keenly focused team in terms of Sales, Quality and Profitability. Displays initiative and a positive outlook to all challenges, ideas generator, decisive and highly adaptable to change. Extensive experience and knowledge of both general and sales management with an in-depth understanding of the people business.

ACHIEVEMENTS

Developed teams of managers monitoring both personal performance and that of the sales units, ensuring objectives achieved together with quality and service standards being maintained.

Created a competitive team spirit whereby individual and collective performance was recognised. Provided league tables, instigated competitions, produced interesting and varied communication formats.

Energised Team, created environment ensuring national Sales Campaigns were tackled enthusiastically with success being achieved and measured in improving performance position.

Appointed and managed new Direct Sales Force including sales meetings, one-to-one coaching and field visits. Developed and nurtured relationships with sales units to achieve common business objectives, resulting in business levels being increased by 140% over a 6-month period.

Produced quarterly/annual business plans to ensure focus and direction to achieving business and quality objectives.

Instigated and developed a programme and systems for achieving Total Quality Management resulting in customer service complaints being reduced by 28% in 3 months.

Responsible for staff recruitment at junior management level. Disciplinary matters and general personnel responsibilities including managing staff budgets.

Responsible for quarterly/annual appraisal process whereby individuals recognise critical success factors which are incorporated within a personal Development Plan.

Involved with the training of staff both within units and at Area Training Centre. Follow-up process adopted to ensure training benefits maximised.

Took part in strategic projects from inception to final presentation enabling project management skills to be developed to the full.

Conducted regular meetings and one-to-one discussions using consultative planning approach agreeing action points to ensure progress.

CAREER PROGRESSION   1965–1992   **Stable Building Society**

1991 – 1992	**Area Sales Manager**	Midlands
	Responsible for 16 Managers, 135 staff.	
	Reported to the Area Sales Director.	
1989 – 1991	**Regional Sales Manager**	East Midlands
	Responsible for 8 Managers, 4 Direct Sales.	
1988 – 1989	**Regional Manager**	Coventry
1987 – 1988	**Assistant Regional Manager**	Coventry
1986 – 1987	**Branch Manager**	Harrogate
1979 – 1986	**Branch Manager**	Crewe
1973 – 1979	**Branch Manager**	Maidenhead
1968 – 1973	**Junior Management/Senior Clerical**	Various Locations

PERSONAL DEVELOPMENT

March 1989	Sundridge Park Management Centre
November 1989	Peters Management Consultants (Sales Training)
December 1987	Ashridge Management College
	Extensive Internal Training covering a wide range of topics.

ADDITIONAL INFORMATION

Married – 1 child (19)
Fellow Chartered Building Society Institute.
School Governor/Chairman of Charitable Trust.
Past member of Round Table, holding a number of offices including Chairman.

INTERESTS

Gardening, golf, badminton, stamp collecting, trying to keep fit.

PETER RADLETT

14 GREENVIEW
CENTRAL MILTON KEYNES
MK98 89MK
TEL: (987) 676767

CAREER PROFILE

Experienced and versatile manager with strong leadership skills. Knowledge of high technology applied to a variety of product-based organisations. Commercially aware. Adept at introducing change either in the organisation or by the introduction of capital investment, and who recognises that high productivity is only achieved through a knowledgeable and motivated team.

ACHIEVEMENTS

* Implemented a £4 million investment programme on a greenfield site through the installation and commissioning of 4 discreet product lines
* Implemented capital investment programme to reduce reliance on external suppliers of key components
* Introduced the concept of Operator Process Control by use of a series of training modules
* Recruited, trained and motivated the production team to develop and grow the business
* Implemented new production planning routines to reduce generation of works documentation from 10 days to 4 days
* Reduced inventory holding on major product lines from 15 weeks to 5 weeks
* Developed, through training, line management supervision
* Reduced losses by improved monitoring and feedback to suppliers

CAREER HISTORY

1991 – Present	OPMKS Ltd, Milton Keynes – Manufacturing Manager, responsible to Operations Director, for all aspects of manufacture for photographic enlargers in a vertically integrated organisation.
1989 – 1991	TISSUE Group, Hemel Hempstead – Production Manager, responsible to Operations Director, for all aspects of manufacture for Tissue Culture Products.
1987 – 1989	VENTILATORS Ltd, High Wycombe – Production Manager, responsible to Manufacturing Director, for line production, line planning and stock control.
1982 – 1987	HYDRAULIC MOTORS Ltd, High Wycombe – Manufacturing Manager, responsible to General Manager, for Purchasing, Production Planning, Stock Control, Production Engineering, Machining Assembly and Despatch.

PETER RADLETT ctd

EDUCATION AND QUALIFICATIONS

1970 – 1972	Hemel Hempstead Polytechnic - HND in Mechanical Engineering
1984	High Wycombe College of Further Education – Certificate in Computing Studies
1985	High Wycombe College of Further Education – Member, Institute of Industrial Managers (IIM)

MANAGEMENT TRAINING

1983	Guardian Business School – Accountancy for non-Financial Managers
1990–1991	PRAGMATICA – Leadership and Decision-making Skills

INTERESTS
Squash, home improvements, walking and classic cars

ROBERT GREEN

IVYBRIDGE HOUSE,
MANCHESTER ROAD,
STALYBRIDGE
M99 99M

TEL: (669) 99991

****

An experienced Manager with Design, Technical and Sales skills. Has designed numerous products including Bedroom/Kitchen ranges and Occasional furniture. Prepared Technical Details of products including packaging. Handled numerous Sales enquiries/contracts, liaising with clients at all levels. Assembled and fitted products including Bedroom and Kitchen ranges.

****

ACHIEVEMENTS

* Designed many successful products for mail order and high street clients including a new bedroom range by Bedroom Sellers and Housefitters.
* Handled door contracts with national companies from enquiries through to production.
* Designed and erected exhibition stands both in the UK and abroad.

EXPERIENCE

Bedrooms Ltd   1989 – 1994
Manchester   **Development Manager**
Responsible for design and development of all the company's new products from conception through to production. This involved accurate preparation of production drawings using Autocad, material and fittings specifications, packing design and instruction leaflets. On the sales side I handled all the company's incoming door and component enquiries, liaising closely with customers on technical matters. I had a staff of 5 and was responsible for CNC Programming and the Development Workshop.

Components Ltd   1973 – 1989
Lancashire   **Development Manager**
Commenced my career as Design Draughts Person working my way to Development Manager on leaving. I was responsible for all aspects of design and development work including aesthetic, economic and production considerations. Was required to draw up and meet planning time tables; producing sketches and cost for short-listed designs. Was involved with presentation and selling of product, pricing and quotations. I produced detailed customer assembly leaflets and was responsible for a busy development workshop.

Shell Oil Refinery   1970 – 1973
Cheshire   **Process Operator**
Responsible for efficient running of Petrol refinery plant.

ROBERT GREEN ctd

Bolton Borough Council   **1965 – 1970**
Bolton   Clerk/Draughts Person
I gained experience in several different aspects of a Council department, including printing, preparation of art work, and furniture where I planned kitchen layouts for Domestic Science rooms in schools and colleges.

EDUCATION AND TRAINING

Bolton Technical High School
GCE 'O' levels in English Language, Mathematics and Technical Drawing.

Manchester College of Furniture
Trained for Design and Construction of Furniture.

FIRA
Various day courses and seminars

College of Further Education
Bolton
City & Guilds in Computer Aided Draughting and Design using Autocad.

HOBBIES AND PASTIMES

I am a married man with two children. My interests include most sports but particularly fishing. I do a lot of walking, living close to moorland. I maintain and improve our house and do most of my own car maintenance.

CATHERINE SCARLET

14 Severn View,
Bristol
BS99 9AA
Tel: 1234 56789 (home), 1234 98765 (office)

Finance Director with general management, company development and acquisition experience combined with practical operating skills in the Investment Banking, Broking, Chemical Processing and Retail Distribution industries. Special abilities include:

* Managing change; turning round underperforming activities.
* Forming, managing and motivating teams; developing individuals.
* Developing profitable relationships, negotiating business deals.
* Analysing, evaluating and managing company aquisitions.

CAREER LOTSACASH   INVESTMENT BANK GROUP
Operations Director, Capital Markets & Treasury, 1987 – 1994

Responsible for efficient operation of Capital Markets/Treasury financial control, settlements and computer operations. 100 staff, budget £10m.
* Specifically recruited to turn-round ineffective accounting, computer and treasury control system.
* Re-built teams, improved staff quality and training, reduced staff and overtime without disruption, significantly improved management information and operating efficiency.
* Investigated and negotiated joint-venture arrangements in Europe.

BROKING INTERNATIONAL PLC, 1978 – 1986
Commercial Director, 1986
Responsible for the London based broking businesses. T/O £75m, profit £9m, 500 staff.
* Conducted start-up of German bond-broking business.

Financial Director, Management and Securities Division, 1981 – 1986

Responsible for advising the Board on worldwide financial and related management matters. T/O £113m, profit £22m. 90 staff.
* Close involvement with acquisitions in UK, USA, Germany, Luxembourg, Hong Kong, Singapore and Australia and with subsequent business development.

Group Financial Controller, 1979 – 1981
* Improved full range of management systems and controls in media advertising and broking activities.
  Contributions in the job led to promotion to Financial Director.

STACKEM HIGH STORES
PA to Chairman, Retail Stores Division, 1977 – 1978
* Investigated, recommended and implemented the integration of 2 stores groups.

SPRINGY SOFAS LTD
Managing Director, 1976
* Planned and brought new factory to full production of moulded urethane components.
* Developed market strategy and customer base of Group. T/O £3m profit £160k.

QUALIFICATIONS
BA Accountancy and Law 2/1, University of Bristol 1968
CA gained with Price Waterhouse, 1971

PERSONAL
Age 46 years. Married, 2 children. Health excellent. Interests – family, antiques, aerobics, Greek Mythology.

JANET WAITE

58 Desmond Road,
London
NW19 9DE
Tel: (081) 055 5656

PROFILE

An effective personnel generalist with skills in team building and gaining commitment from Senior Management through persuasion.

Enjoys deadlines and performs well under pressure. Gives whole-hearted commitment to a task and displays a high degree of tenacity and resilience when facing difficult situations.

Outside of the work environment enjoys being stretched and, for example, has, in the last few years, taken up skiing, windsurfing and paragliding.

CAREER

VERY WEALTHY BANKS (INVESTMENTS) PLC   1986 – Present
(Based in the City with 2,500 employees in a highly IT oriented environment).

PERSONNEL MANAGER   1990 – Present
SETTLEMENT SERVICES DIVISION
A strongly generalist role, responsible for the provision of an effective professional service to c900 staff. Managing a team of 6 personnel staff. My achievements in this role have been:
* Following significant cutbacks, selected to contribute to re-structuring.
* Charged with the task of detailed project planning and execution for the transfer of personnel activities back to line managers.

PERSONNEL MANAGER   1988 – 1990
INFORMATION TECHNOLOGY

Managing a team of 5 staff (including 3 professional personnel officers) covering strongly Systems Development oriented client areas, c550 staff. My achievements in this position were:-
* Worked with the senior management team to revise job roles and restructure a) the Systems Development and Support department resulting in the reduction of 30 staff and b) the Management Services department resulting in the reduction of 50 jobs.
* Established a new personnel team of 5 from scratch; recruited, analysed training needs and coached for their improved job performance through regular meetings and improved communications. Heightened team contribution and helped them to develop in their own roles.
* Implemented psychometric testing to determine analytical skills and assessment centre techniques to clarify project management potential, ensuring the cost effective application of training programmes.
* Successfully implemented the appraisal policy within client area, running courses and successfully working to overcome management resistance to objective setting.

PRINCIPAL PERSONNEL OFFICER   1987 – 1988
BUSINESS DEVELOPMENT DEPARTMENT

In a predominantly Sales and Marketing environment managed 3 staff, in a generalist role serving staff in the South East, UK Regional Offices and New York, but also with emphasis on recruitment and remuneration.

* Gained acceptance to the establishment of career paths for Business Development department staff involving progress through Customer Support, UK Sales, International Sales and the New York office.

* Creative and analytical approach to Recruitment into a number of key roles, according to a specification which required a unique combination of Financial Services, Computer Industry and Sales/Marketing expertise.

SENIOR PERSONNEL OFFICER   1986 – 1987

A generalist role, covering the Systems Development and Sales and Marketing department. Particularly involving recruitment and development (Graduate and YTS); and experience in HAY based job evaluation. Achievements in this position were:-

* Sold new salary review concepts to line managers and worked with them in resolving the remuneration level problems which were leading to high turnover of specialist staff.

* Initiated an in-house recruitment event to appeal to computer scientists, gained the commitment of the senior management to participate in the event and achieved recruitment targets.

BIG BOAT BUILDERS, RESEARCH & DEVELOPMENT   1984 – 1986

(Research, development and production of electronic equipment, 2,500 staff)

SENIOR PERSONNEL OFFICER – RECRUITMENT

Responsible for the recruitment of professional, technical, manual, clerical and secretarial staff. Involved in the recruitment of graduates and professional engineers. Achievements in the position were:-

* Became the driving force behind the use of Psychometric Testing for the recruitment of specialist, high value staff. By means of presentations to Senior Management gained acceptance for this approach.

* Ran a series of 'walk in interviews' to attract scarce technical skills and validated its cost effectiveness.

CAR PARTS LTD   1980-1984

(Manufacture and distribution of automotive parts, approx. 2,500 staff)
Successive appointments in this heavily unionised environment – Graduate Trainee, Salaries & Records Administrator, Personnel Officer, Systems Co-ordinator, Recruitment & Salaries Adviser.

ELECTRONIC SWITCHING LTD   1978 - 1979

Import/Export Sales Co-ordinator.

EDUCATION & TRAINING

Member of The Institute of Personnel Management (1989).
BSc Combined Hons Degree in Science (Zoology/Geography).

Psychometric Testing

Registered user of Thomas International (Personality Profile), Kostic PAPI (Perception & Preference Inventory), Saville & Holdsworth (Aptitude Tests).

PERSONAL

AGE: 36. Single. Interests include: Windsurfing, skiing, hill walking, watching motor racing, keep Siamese cats and enjoy theatre.

Application forms

The mode in which the inevitable comes to pass is through effort.

OLIVER WENDELL HOLMES

What an imposition; you spend all of that time writing your CV, spot an ad in the newspaper for a job that sounds perfect and you ring to ask for details: They send you an information pack and an application form. Why should **you** now waste time completing an application form?

It would be much easier to fill in your name and address at the top of the application form and write, 'please see attached CV' – you might get away with it, you probably won't!

Organisations use application forms for two main reasons:

1. To collect 'standard information' on all candidates, so that the person doing the initial screening can easily compare candidates against each other and the job.
2. So that candidates are 'forced' to provide important information, e.g., a CV may simply show 'full driving licence'. The response to a question on an application form, 'Give details of any driving licence endorsements', may reveal '9 penalty points; 3 x speeding'.

Looked at from one viewpoint, an application form is a chore; from a positive viewpoint, it is your perfectly targeted CV!

COMPLETING APPLICATION FORMS

- Read the form before writing anything.
- Take a photocopy of the blank form to use for drafting your answers.
- Complete the form as requested. Black ink and block capitals doesn't mean blue ink, no matter how dark, and hieroglyphics!
- If you need to expand any of the sections on to extra pages, write your name and job applied for, at the top of each page.
- Match your application to the job: review the job advertisement and any information you have received on the job and match your application to the job.
- Answer all of the questions.
- Explain any gaps in your career.

- Maximise the 'Other Information' opportunity by making a positive 'you' statement – see Activity 29, 'Selection Interviews', – 'Tell me about yourself', (page 152).

- Use feature and benefit statements to relate your past experience to the skills and qualities they are looking for – see Activity 23 'Selling Yourself' (below).

- Don't include any negatives about yourself – this is not the place to be self-effacing

- Telephone referees before putting them on the application. First, as a courtesy, but second, to help them to help you by bringing out your best points when they give a reference. You want them to emphasise particularly those of your skills which are most relevant to the job.

- Proof read, proof read, proof read – and get someone else to do it.

- Photocopy the completed form – so that you know what you've said when you are invited for interview and to add to your brag-box!

- Use first-class postage, or if the organisation is local, make an opportunity to 'be in the area' and deliver it by hand (in the same clothes that you would wear for an interview). You never know, you may even get a chance to meet the recruiter, or at least his or her secretary – an opportunity to make a positive impression, distinguish yourself from the competition and increase the memorability of your application!

Activity 23

Selling myself

What we hope ever to do with ease, we must learn first to do with diligence
SAMUEL JOHNSON

When you're actively job-hunting you are constantly selling yourself whether by letter, telephone or in an interview.

Contrary to what you might think 'selling' isn't only about charm, a smile and a pleasant personality; these are part of it, but the selling process goes far beyond.

Most experts would agree that the basic core of any selling process involves the following:

Beforehand:

Objective Setting	Identifying early what you hope to get out of the contact.

During:

Presenting Opening Benefits	Getting quickly to the point so that the other person can see what's in it for them
Probing for Needs	Using 'How, Why, What, When, Where, and Who' questions to help you understand requirements.
Presenting Benefits	Helping the other person to see the relevance of what you have to offer.
Overcoming Objections	Outweighing any reservations they might have with the benefits you can offer.
Closing	Ending the contact with an agreement of a positive outcome.

PRESENTING BENEFITS

The process of presenting benefits is one which many people find difficult, so let's have a look at what's involved.

Features → Advantages → Benefits

People buy products or services not for what they are, but for what they can do for them. In the same way, companies recruit employees not for **who or what they are**, but **for what they bring to the company and what they can do for the company**.

WHAT'S THE BENEFIT OF BENEFITS?

I bought my computer with a 200 megabyte hard disk because it meant that I wouldn't have to waste time loading and reloading programmes. **BENEFIT – I save time!**

I bought an answerphone with a remote interrogation facility, so that when I stay away from home, I can still keep in touch with my business contacts. **BENEFIT – I keep in touch and don't miss out on business opportunities.**

Benefit statements turn your gobbledygook into language which the other person can understand and is relevant to them.

By using benefit statements you will help the recruiter to understand any technical jargon you may be using and help them see the relevance of what you've done before the job you're being interviewed for.

Remember, in recruitment the recruiter is a 'Customer' who is deciding whether to 'buy' your service for their company.

Feature	Advantage	Benefit
A description of product or service	Says what the feature does	Answers 'what's in it for me?'
A fact or characteristic	Says what the feature means	Answers what features and advantages will ultimately mean to user.
A property or attribute of a product or service	Says what the feature will do	Gives the value of worth that the buyer will get from the product or service.
'Because (of) ...'	'You can ...'	'Which means that ...'

The following exercises will help you to develop benefit statements for yourself.

Identifying benefits for a product/service

Choose something that you have bought recently. Write down 4 features in the 'FEATURE' section below. Now turn each feature into advantages and benefits (one feature can often give rise to a large number of benefits).

FEATURE What it is	ADVANTAGE What it does	BENEFIT What it means
1.		
2.		
3.		
4.		
Because (of) ...	You can ...	Which means that ...

Identifying benefits for me

Identify four of your achievements that you are proud of and write them in the 'FEATURE' section. Convert your features to advantages and benefits for your target job.

FEATURE What have I done What are my achievements	ADVANTAGE What I will be able to do	BENEFIT What it means to you
Because (of) ...	You/I can ...	Which means that ...

At the end of each statement ask yourself 'So what?' to challenge the relevance of what you say to the recruiter.

Use these notepads to summarise your learning points as you complete activities in *I Can Do That!*

Assertiveness and interpersonal skills

Make the most of yourself, for that is all there is for you.
RALPH WALDO EMERSON

Assertiveness skills are very important in many situations; by being assertive you are letting people know what you want, need or prefer in a way which is acceptable to both you and them. Put simply, assertiveness is about getting what you want without upsetting anyone!

In your jobsearch you'll need to be assertive if you're going to persuade people to give up time for networking interviews, send you company information or contact their contacts.

DIFFERENCES BETWEEN ACQUIESCENT, ASSERTIVE AND AGGRESSIVE BEHAVIOUR

Acquiescent	Assertive	Aggressive
You: hope that you will get what you want sit on your feelings rely on others to guess what you want	**You:** ask for what you want directly and openly ask for what you want appropriately have rights ask confidently and without undue anxiety	**You:** try to get what you want in any way that works often cause bad feelings in others threaten, cajole, manipulate, use sarcasm, conflict
You Don't: ask for what you want express your feelings often get what you want upset people get noticed	**You Don't:** violate other people's rights expect other people magically to know what you want freeze with anxiety	**You Don't:** respect that other people have a right to get their needs met look for situations in which you both might be able to get what you want ('win-win situations')

Which column do you fit in for most of the time … yes, I know everyone knows they should be in the centre column, but **are you**? If you aren't, set yourself three improvement goals to develop your assertiveness skills to help you to shift into the centre column.

Assertiveness goals

1. _____

2. _____

3. _____

Understanding and recognising assertiveness is a major step in helping you to develop your interpersonal and influencing skills.

There are two other important factors however:

1. How you prefer to behave with other people.
2. How the people you interact with like others to behave towards them.

For example, some people are the life and soul of the party, dress flamboyantly and speak in loud, fast voices; get two of them together and it's almost a competition to see who can burst the other's eardrums! Try approaching one of these people in a polite, mild-mannered and factual way and you're unlikely to make an impression.

Other people like to conduct business in a very formal way, they're abrupt and to the point and only interested in 'the bottom line'. Approach a meeting with these people with a barrage of questions about family, hobbies and what they did during the weekend, and you've probably burned up 80 per cent of the time they've allocated for the meeting!

SOCIAL STYLES

How can you ensure that you approach people in the correct way?

Knowing about 'Social Styles', developed by Merrill and Reid, is very useful. In the Social Styles Model there are four basic 'styles' or preferred ways of interacting with others.

Merrill and Reid believe that a person's Social Style is a way of coping with others. People become most comfortable with that style, in themselves and others. Understanding your own style and those of others can help in making meetings more productive: the main objective of Social Styles is to help people to develop versatility in dealing with others.

A person's Social Style is measured in relation to three behavioural dimensions: **assertiveness**, **responsiveness** and **versatility**.

The assertiveness scale

The assertive scale measures the degree to which a person is seen as attempting to influence the thoughts, decisions or actions of others, either directly by '**tell**' behaviour or indirectly by questioning, '**ask**' behaviour.

Tell behaviour: Risk-taking, fast-paced, challenging.
Ask behaviour: Co-operative, deliberate actions, minimising risks.

The responsiveness scale

The responsive scale measures the degree to which a person either openly expresses their feelings or controls their feelings. The ends of the scale are '**control**' and '**emote**'.

Control behaviour: Disciplined, serious, cool.
Emote behaviour: Relationship-oriented, open, warm.

The two scales combine to give a two-dimensional model of behaviour, shown below, which will help you to understand how you are perceived by others. The dimensions of behaviour will also help you to plan how you can deal more effectively with people of different Social Styles.

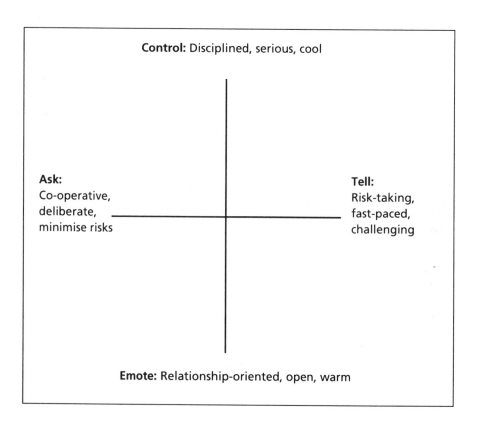

MY SOCIAL STYLE

A very simple way of identifying your Social Style is to copy the dimensions of the behaviour model from the above box on to a number of pieces of paper. Now ask people who know you well, to plot your behaviour as they see it. Explain the two axes to them and then ask them to put a cross, **first on the horizontal scale and then on the vertical scale**. Try not to influence their decision; better still ask them to do it anonymously.

If you have a majority of crosses on 'control' and 'ask' then your behaviour is seen as analytical. If on 'Control' and 'tell' you are seen as a Driver.

If you are 'emote' and 'ask' then you are seen as an Amiable. If you are 'Emote' and 'tell' you are seen as an Expressive.

THE SOCIAL STYLES MODEL

	Control	
Ask	**Analytical**	**Driver**	Tell
	Amiable	**Expressive**	
	Emote	

The Social Styles Model is not about 'putting people into boxes', it is a way of plotting two dimensions of behaviour which then give us patterns to help our interpersonal skills.

By knowing about your own Social Style and recognising Social Styles in others you can improve the effectiveness of your meetings with others.

The table on page 134 summarises the characteristics of each of the Social Styles.

CHARACTERISTICS OF EACH SOCIAL STYLE

Analyticals	Drivers
• Concerned with being organised, having all the facts and being careful before taking action. • Need is to be accurate and to be right. • Precise, orderly and methodical, and conform to standard operating procedures, organisational rules, and historical ways of doing things. • Have a slow reaction time and work more slowly and carefully than Drivers. • Perceived as serious, industrious, persistent, and exacting • Are task-oriented. • Use facts and data. • Tend to speak slowly. • Lean back and use their hands infrequently. • Do not make direct eye contact. • Control their facial expressions. • Others may see them as stuffy, indecisive, critical, picky and moralistic. • Comfortable in positions in which they can check facts and figures and be sure they are right. • Neat/well organised offices. • In times of stress, analyticals tend to avoid conflict.	• Action and goal-oriented. • Need to see results. • Have a quick reaction time and are decisive, independent, disciplined, practical and efficient. • Use facts and data. • Speak and act quickly. • Lean forward and point and make direct eye contact. • Bodily posture is rigid. • Controlled facial expressions. • Do not want to waste time on personal talk or preliminaries and can be perceived by other styles as dominating or harsh and severe in pursuit of a goal. • Comfortable in positions of power and control. • Businesslike offices with certificates and commendations on the wall. • In times of stress, drivers may become autocratic.

Amiable	Expressives
• Need co-operation, personal security, and acceptance. • Uncomfortable with and will avoid conflict. • Value personal relationship, helping others, and being liked. • Some amiables will sacrifice their own desires to win approval from others. • Prefer to work with other people in a team effort, rather than individually. • Have an unhurried reaction time and little concern with effecting change. • Friendly, supportive, respectful, willing dependable, and agreeable. • Are people-oriented. • Use opinions and stories rather than facts and data. • Speak slowly and softly. • Use more vocal inflection than Drivers or Analyticals. • Lean back while talking and do not make direct eye contact. • Have a casual posture and an animated expression. • Perceived by other styles as comforting, unsure, pliable, dependent, and awkward. • 'Homely' offices – family photographs, plants, etc. • An amiable's reaction to stress is to comply with others.	• Enjoy involvement, excitement, and interpersonal action. • Are sociable, stimulating, and enthusiastic and are good at involving and motivating others. • Idea-oriented. • Have little concern for routine and are future-oriented. • Have a quick reaction time. • Need to be accepted by others. • Tend to be spontaneous, outgoing, energetic, and friendly. • Focused on people rather than on tasks. • Use opinions and stories rather than facts and data. • Speak and act quickly; vary vocal inflection. • Lean forward, point, and make direct eye contact. • Use their hands when talking. • Have a relaxed bodily posture and an animated expression. Their feelings often show in their faces. • Perceived by others as excitable, impulsive, undisciplined, dramatic, manipulative, ambitious, overly reactive, and egotistical. • Disorganised offices may have leisure equipment like golf clubs or tennis racquets. • Under stressful conditions, expressives tend to resort to personal attack.

VERSATILITY – MAKING SOCIAL STYLES WORK FOR YOU

First of all it is important to recognise that **there is no best style**. Merrill and Reid found that around 25 per cent of the adult population belonged to each Social Style. They also found people from each Social Style at all levels within organisations.

The third dimension and the key to using Social Styles is versatility. Statistically, around a quarter of the population have a similar Social Style to yours and so you will find that you are naturally comfortable with them.

Some people are naturally very versatile and are able to adapt easily to the needs of other people; others are less so. **By developing your versatility skills, you will be able to relate effectively with a greater number of people**.

The people whom you probably find it most difficult to relate to naturally are your 'diagonal opposites' on the matrix. Study the characteristics of your 'diagonally opposite' Social Style.

Make some notes in the box below on how you can adapt your behaviour temporarily, i.e., improve your versatility, next time you meet your 'diagonal opposite'. For example, Analyticals may need to 'warm up' when dealing with Expressives and be prepared to discuss business (network) over a pie and a pint or in the gym – just because the surroundings are informal doesn't make the information any less important. Expressives need to be specific in their contacts with Analyticals; be precise about what you want and you'll find they have a wealth of knowledge, but give them time to gather it. Amiables need to get to the point quickly when dealing with Drivers – all that chitchat about family and hobbies is lost on the Driver. Similarly the Driver needs to slow things down when meeting an Amiable in order to develop a trusting relationship.

> **Improving my versatility with my opposite social style:**
>
> _____
>
> _____
>
> _____

THREE FINAL GOLDEN RULES

1. Person #1 is not person #2 – We are all different and individual.
2. Person #1 today is different from person #1 tomorrow – we all have our moods, both good and bad.
3. We can never know **everything** about a person or situation.

Active listening skills

He who talks much cannot talk well.

CARLO GOLDONI

Most of us are poor listeners ... 'sorry did you say something ...'? I said most of us are poor listeners!

We are so concerned with what we are going to ask or say, that we ignore or miss a lot of what the other person says.

Improving your active listening skills will help you to collect valuable information in your research interviews, when you're networking and when you are being interviewed for a job.

STAGES IN A NETWORKING INTERVIEW

1. Establish a relationship.
2. Encourage the other person to talk.
3. Reflect what the other person has said.
4. Summarise the key ideas you have got from the meeting.
5. Thank them for their time.

Look at the ten commandments of active listening below. How many 'sins' did you commit in your last networking interview?

THE TEN COMMANDMENTS OF ACTIVE LISTENING

1. JUDGEMENT EVALUATION – Thou shalt not judge nor evaluate until thou has understood!
2. NON-CRITICAL INFERENCE – Thou shalt not infer thoughts, facts, or ideas in addition to those stated; avoid embellishment!
3. PLURAL INFERENCE – Thou shalt not attribute thine own thoughts and ideas to the speaker!
4. LACK OF ATTENTION – Thou shalt not permit thy thoughts to stray nor thy attention to wander!
5. ATTITUDE – Thou shalt not close thy mind to others
6. WISHFUL HEARING – Thou shalt not permit they heart to rule thy mind!
7. SEMANTICS – Thou shalt not interpret words and phrases except as they are interpreted by the speaker!
8. EXCESSIVE TALKING – Thou shalt not become infatuated with the sound of thine own voice!
9. LACK OF HUMILITY – Thou shalt not consider thyself too good to learn from any person!
10. FEAR – Thou shalt not fear improvement, correction, or change!

IMPROVING YOUR ACTIVE LISTENING SKILLS

Non-verbal listening skills

You can communicate that you are actively listening by showing that you are paying full attention and not just waiting for your turn to speak, for example, by:

- Looking at the person
- Nodding your head
- Facial expressions, e.g., raised eyebrows, a smile
- Attentive body posture, e.g., sitting forward

Verbal listening skills

There are a number of ways which will indicate clearly not only that you are listening but also interested in what the other person has to say:

- Rephrasing in your own words, e.g., *'So what you are saying is ...'*
- Summarising key points.
- Encouraging the other person to continue, e.g., *'That's interesting, tell me more ...'*
- Asking questions for further information or clarification, e.g.,

    Why do you say that?

    Why is that important to you?

    What do you mean by that?

    What does that mean to you?

    Would you explain that further?

    How does that relate to what you said before?

    Could you give me an example of that?

    Can you define or describe that?

If you remember Rudyard Kipling's reply when he was asked how he came to develop such a wide knowledge, you won't go too far wrong. He said:

> *I keep six honest serving men*
> *(they taught me all I knew);*
> *Their names are **what** and **why** and **when!***
> *and **how** and **where** and **who**.*

ATTITUDE

The chief requirement for active listening is to have 'room' for others; if we are preoccupied with our own thoughts, ideas and views, we are not mentally 'available' to listen effectively.

When listening, it is helpful really to try to understand the other person's view, without superimposing your own views or judgements prematurely – a major block to active listening.

Back to 'The Ten Commandments of Active Listening'!

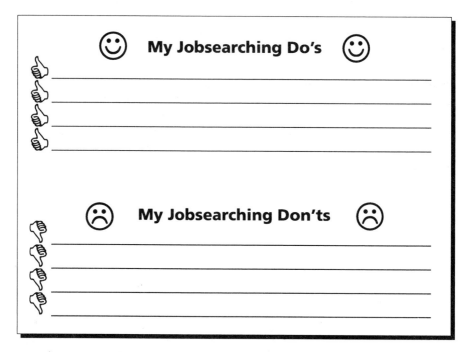

Use these notepads to summarise your learning points as you complete activities in *I Can Do That!*

First impressions that last

There is new strength, repose of mind and inspiration in fresh apparel.
ELLA WHEELER WILCOX

When we communicate with people in a face to face setting we use two principal ways to transmit our message: words (content and voice tone) and body language.

Our **'Word Message'** is made up from **the words** spoken and **the way words are spoken**.

The **'body language message'** is the message we project through our **gestures, actions and the** way we dress.

Now interviews are all about talking, usually one to one with another person, aren't they? You would be forgiven then, for thinking that when you first meet someone you are going to capture their attention, provided that you have something interesting to talk about! It may surprise you to know that a number of studies have shown that the majority (around 80 per cent) of the messages we transmit to other people are through our body language.

We have spent a good deal of time throughout the rest of this book concentrating on what should be **said** in interviews. In this activity we will look at techniques you can use so that your body language projects the impression that you would want it to project.

STEREOTYPES

Whether you like it or not most people label others within the first few moments of meeting them. As much as 90 per cent of a person's impression of you is made in the first four minutes. Some of your initial impact comes from what you say but the majority of your impact comes from the way you behave and the way you dress – the other person stereotypes you.

To give you an example: in most western films what does the 'Bad Guy' look like? Moustache/unshaven, dark/black clothing and a black hat. He is easy to recognise – Lee Van Cleef hasn't played the part of a schoolteacher or parish priest, as far as I can remember!

Butch Cassidy and the Sundance Kid confused our stereotyping by wearing camel-coloured clothes and being fresh faced and clean shaven (the slightly more villainous one wore a moustache). By breaking the stereotype, two outright criminals endeared themselves to millions of viewers.

Speak to most rational people and they will argue quite strongly that they 'always keep an open mind when they meet new people' and they are 'never quick to form an opinion'.

I understand the sentiment. In reality, I'm afraid it's not true.

Try this. Quickly imagine:

A Secretary	now
A Glazier	now
A School-meals Assistant	now
A Sales Manager	now

What sexes were the people? What were they wearing?

Was the Glazier wearing a dress or a skirt? Was the School-meals Assistant wearing a suit, or was he wearing a blazer? Were you guilty of stereotyping?

You will stand a far better chance of getting the job you want if the image you project, through your body language, creates the right impact. In those vital first four minutes, you need to show that you fit into the stereotype.

I know that some people are very uncomfortable with what I have just said ... 'What about freedom of choice' ... 'No I'm afraid what they see is what they get' ... 'If they don't like me as I am then I'd rather go elsewhere.' If this is the way you feel then fine, I respect your opinions. What I will say however, is that **you may be shortening your options**.

My target job

What is your stereotype of someone doing your target job? How do they behave? How are they dressed? What does their body language say? Make a few notes in the space below.

_____

_____

_____

POSITIVE IMPACT: BODY LANGUAGE

Dress yourself in a dark blue pinstriped suit, a white cotton shirt with double cuffs, a 'military' striped tie, black lace-up shoes and wear a plain faced watch. (The female equivalent is the same with no tie, a white cotton blouse and black court shoes.) Your body language is about as persuasive and influential as your dress can let you be (No. 1 Dress).

Studies carried out by IBM found that people dressed as I have just described were 40 per cent more believable than people who were 'less powerfully' dressed.

I'll leave it to you to guess how IBM sales people dress.

The less believable end of the scale is the camel-coloured suit, brown shoes and coloured shirt (No. 5 Dress). While higher up come the light greys (No. 4 Dress) with dark greys even higher (No. 3 Dress). Watch the politicians and other public figures on television to see what effect the way they are dressed has on their 'believability quotient' with you.

It is impossible to generalise and give a definitive 'This is what you should wear for interviews', since all jobs have different requirements, but the following will be useful.

- Decide where on the 1-5 scale your dress should be appropriate to the job. Lovely as that new suit is (you know the one you bought for your brother's wedding), ask yourself if it is right for the job interview?

- Clean, well-pressed clothes in good repair – there aren't any buttons missing from the shirt/blouse you're planning to wear, are there?

- Wear some perfume or aftershave – but make sure it's not too overpowering. Be subtle.

- If you keep pets, brush your clothes thoroughly. Those cat hairs will start to look three feet long if you spot them on your clothes in the middle of an interview!

- Polish your shoes until you can see your face in them – not suede ones!

- If you're carrying a briefcase give it a polish.

- **For men**: earrings and white socks are a turn-off for most recruiters.

- **For women**: If you're wearing a new skirt, try the sit-down test when you buy it – is it too short? I once interviewed a young lady who sat through the whole interview with her top coat on her lap. She'd bought a new skirt for the interview and only realised how short it was when she sat down in it for the first time on the bus, on the way to the interview – too late!

  Beware of silk shirts and blouses – perspiration can really spoil their smart appearance.

  If you wear nail polish use 'neutral colours'.

  If you wear jewellery ask yourself if it is appropriate or too loud.

  Carry a spare pair of stockings/tights in your bag.

  Take only one bag with you into the interview. Fumbling between a handbag and a briefcase can make you look disorganised and reduces your confidence.

- *Colours*: A number of my friends have benefited from 'having their colours done', by taking advice on colours and tones to suit their skin and hair colour. The downside is that it's quite expensive – you may need to change your wardrobe! The positive side is that most of them feel it was beneficial. A cheaper alternative is a video, 'Discover Your Colours' (addresses in Appendix).

In addition to standing tall, smiling and being warm and friendly towards interviewers, the following will help you to send out positive messages.

- *A Handshake*: rightly or wrongly people read all kinds of interpretations into people's handshakes, from the limp lettuce, non-assertive, to the knuckle-crushing bully! A firm, but gently 'middle ground' handshake is usually appropriate to start and end interviews.

- *Don't crowd the interviewer's personal space*: In western society 4-6 feet is about as near as you should get to someone in an interview.

- *Hold eye contact*, but don't stare.

- *Mirror the interviewer's body gestures*: if the interviewer crosses their legs, do the same. If they raise their hand to their face, copy their gesture to produce a 'mirror image'. By this method you are telling the interviewer, that you are in agreement with their ideas or attitudes. (Make sure that your mirroring is natural, otherwise mirroring will become mimicking!) If you want to observe mirroring, go along to your local pub or bar and watch people making each other feel relaxed, by mirroring.

- *Don't sit with your arms crossed*: they form a physical block or barrier and send out an '*I don't believe you* message.

- *Read the other person's body language.*
  - Pulling or poking their ear – they've heard enough. Move on.
  - Hand clenching or clenching the chair arm – they're not impressed with your answer. Change the subject.
  - Readjusting their cuff/watch strap – they're bored. Move on.
  - Sitting back – they want to listen.
  - Leaning back with hands clasped behind the head, they want you to convince them.
  - Rubbing the chin suddenly – they're interested in what you're saying.
  - Index finger pointing up and resting on the cheek – they're evaluating what your saying.
  - Leaning forward and rubbing hands together – they're very interested in what you're saying.

LAST IMPRESSIONS

A last impression from me!

Don't get so 'hung up' about gestures, actions and dress that you forget about the content of the interview! Watch people in real life or on television for examples of what I'm talking about.

When you attend an interview, a few well-chosen gestures and nicely matched attire will help you to create that perfect impression in the first four minutes.

The way in – finding vacant jobs

The sleeping fox catches no poultry.

BENJAMIN FRANKLIN

There are three kinds of job vacancies. Those which:

- **already exist**, someone has been promoted or left, etc.
- **are about to exist**, as a result of retirement or someone moving on or a company expansion
- **are created**, because your approach convinces the employer that there is a problem to be solved.

THERE ARE TWO WAYS OF JOBSEARCHING

Reactive: You read the vacancies sections in newspapers, journals and the vacancy boards of the Job Centre.

Estimates vary, but many believe that as few as 25 per cent of all job vacancies are ever advertised.

Proactive: You combine your skills as an Inspector Morse-type detective to discover vacancies and your skills as an Anita Roddick/Richard Branson entrepreneur to market yourself so that you get the job.

Persistence and flexibility pays

When I was a 19 year old student, I borrowed the airfare to the United States and enough money for me to exist on for 11 weeks from my parents. (Students do get long holidays don't they!) My travelling companion, Keith, and I arrived in Atlantic City, which is like Blackpool but around ten times bigger, in the middle of the holiday period. We had work permits and were sure that we'd be able to find jobs. We couldn't. American students start their summer holidays before the UK colleges. Every temporary job had gone.

We spent three full days from 7.00 am until 10.00 pm calling at every hotel, restaurant, shop ... anywhere where we thought we could get work.

We took a bus to Philadelphia and spent another day doing the same thing there. But no luck.

We took a bus to Harrisburg. By mid afternoon we had met a clerk at the employment offices who said there were no jobs in Harrisburg, but if we were interested in picking fruit he would take us that night to Gettysburg, where he knew there were jobs.

The next morning at 7.00 am we waited for the bus to arrive to take us to the fruit farm. It didn't arrive. It had been cancelled. No jobs.

The Gettysburg address I had was three thousand miles from home; we knew no one else and had just about enough money to survive for the rest of the trip! Back to knocking on doors. We also wrote a letter to the Editor of the local newspaper saying how much we were enjoying our visit to the USA, but did **anyone** have any work?

In the meantime I managed to get a job – as a dishwasher at a Holiday Inn. Two days later our letter was published and a director of a shoe factory (who was English) rang to offer us jobs. Promotion! I resigned my job as a dishwasher and started at the shoe factory.

Two days after that, I received a call from a Howard Johnson Restaurant asking if I wanted a job as a cook. I explained that I had a daytime job, but was available during the evenings and at weekends. I started that evening.

I now had two jobs. A week later one of the other cooks resigned. I told the Manager that Keith was available. He now had two jobs.

Persistence, flexibility, creativity and networking took the pair of us from being unemployed to giving us jobs that earned us enough money to repay our debts, finance our flights and an eleven-week stay, which included a three week, 11,000 mile tour of the USA!

Reading the appointments section in newspapers is an important part of jobsearching but there are **many** other ways.

PROACTIVE JOB SEARCHING

There are two ways:

Traditional techniques of proactive jobsearching

- Identify potential employers and write to a **named** person; not the personnel manager (unless you're looking for a personnel job), but the person running the department.

- To help in identifying potential employers take a trip to your local library and do some book research. There are literally dozens of directories. A quick phone call can re-confirm a name. When you know which geographical area, industry/public sector you are targeting, ask the librarian for advice on which directories will be most useful. The books will be in the reference section and some of the titles you will find useful will be:

> *The Personnel Manager's Year Book*
> *Kompass Register of British Industry and Commerce*
> *The Times 1000*
> *Who Own Whom?*

Stock Exchange Official Year Book
Directory of British Associations
Kelly's Manufactures and Merchants Directories (Regionalised)

And don't forget about the *Yellow Pages* and other local directories. And also the membership lists of professional bodies, e.g., the Institute of Chartered Accountants in England and Wales, the Law Society, the Institute of Taxation, etc.

There are also industry-specific directories, e.g., *Pharmafile* for healthcare industries.

The list goes on and on – don't be put off. **Ask** for help and be prepared to do some digging!

- Write speculative letters to headhunters and recruitment agencies. Build up your bank of names and addresses from friends and business contacts. Also, scan the newspapers and journals (current and previous editions) for people who work in your target area. An excellent source of names and addresses is the CEPEC Recruitment Guide, (see Appendix for details).

- Contact the Branch Chairperson or Secretary of your professional organisation.

- *Network*: First of all, brainstorm the names of as many friends, acquaintances and business contacts as you can. Telephone them and get to the point quickly. Have three objectives:

  1. **To let them know that you're looking for work** – so that they can keep their eyes and ears open
  2. **To ask them for the names of two of their contacts** whom you might approach
  3. **To ask for their advice** about opportunities/recruitment consultants/journals/ads they might have seen

- *Personal Recommendation*: if you have been made redundant, will your previous Manager write to, or telephone, people in their network to ask if they will meet you? ... **Ask!**

G.O.Y.A. techniques of proactive jobsearching

Get off Your A _ _ _!

- Be prepared to put in **a lot of effort**. Whatever effort you have planned to put into jobsearching, double it to a minimum of twenty hours per week and be prepared for a long journey. You need to put in some long hours. Be prepared to make dozens of phone calls and be prepared to write tens, or even hundreds, of letters of application.

- Target small companies. With a few exceptions, the big companies are contracting while **some** of the smaller ones are growing. Also, in a smaller company you're far more likely to get to see the decision maker. Go there in person.

- Go to visit potential employers. Arrive in reception. Ask for the Manager by name and be ready for a short interview; this is what sales people call a speculative call – of course it doesn't work every time. But if you never do it, then it won't ever work. And you only need it to **really** work once don't you! Be brave, try it!

- Aim to see ten employers each week, either through formal interviews or through speculative calls as described above.

- Visit your old school, college or university, nursing school, etc. People there may be aware of vacancies for people, with the skills or knowledge you have, or they may be able to give you names to add to your network.

- Have lots of 'irons in the fire'. Sometimes when people are jobsearching they 'fall in love' with one vacancy. As the interview process proceeds, they exclude any activity in looking for alternatives. It's almost as if there would be some kind of disloyalty to this potential job.

- Networking in person – wherever possible meet people face to face, rather than on the telephone: for a quick lunch, a meeting in the pub after work, or for a coffee. They'll give you ten times as much information in a one-to one-meeting, as they will in a telephone call.

- If you've been shortlisted for a job and are attending a series of interviews put your heart and soul into it ... but don't do it to the exclusion of all other activities. Keep jobsearching.

- Be creative, brainstorm! Try to think of novel and different techniques of finding out about new jobs. See if your friends can come up with different ways.

Can't be done – don't close your mind! Someone once found out my name and hand-delivered a nicely packaged box to the reception area of the company, where I worked as a personnel manager. The package was endorsed 'perishable – urgent'. It was delivered to me immediately, straight into my office (not buried in an in-tray) and placed on my desk. The contents: two packs of sandwiches from Marks and Spencers, a can of fresh orange juice, a cream cake and even a napkin. A letter in the box, from a young lady, explained that she realised I was a busy person; perhaps if she bought me lunch, the time I had saved could be spent giving her a short interview? When she telephoned me two days later, I spoke to her personally and met her a few days later. She had jumped in front of literally dozens of people. Regrettably, we didn't have any suitable vacancies. If we had, she would have been near the front of the queue ... No, not because she bought lunch for me! But because she was prepared to try something different. It nearly worked. What she did get were some contact names of people in my network.

PS. I'm not suggesting that you now start to feed every potential recruiter! I am simply trying to demonstrate that there are merits in thinking creatively.

A friend of mine who is a partner in a law firm gave me this example.

'When recruiting for a Solicitor we used a headhunter, found an ideal candidate and he turned us down. Then I went to specialist agencies. Lots of CVs, interviews, etc. I turned down one person – not convinced she could develop the business enough. She wrote to me a couple of days later with her ideas for generating further business. I was impressed, had her back for a further interview and she got the job!'

> If you have an interesting jobsearch method you have used, which has worked, write to me (see 'Pass it on' on p. ix) so that we can share it with your fellow jobsearchers.

You may be asking yourself, which jobsearching technique should I use?

My advice is: ALL OF THEM!

☺ **My Jobsearching Do's** ☺

_____

_____

_____

_____

☹ **My Jobsearching Don'ts** ☹

_____

_____

_____

_____

Use these notepads to summarise your learning points as you complete activities in *I can do that!*

Understanding selection criteria

Nothing is really work unless you would rather be doing something else.
JAMES MATTHEW BARRIE

Present yourself well in an interview and you're probably 95 per cent of the way to getting the job! So how do you do it?

Good interviewers work to a plan, using questions to measure/assess you against their ideal profile. They set standards/requirements relating to a variety of factors and decide if these are essential or desirable. The figure on p. 149 shows a typical 'Person Profile Form', used by many recruiters.

HOW THE SELECTION CRITERIA ARE USED

When planning a recruitment project a recruiter will use the 'Person Profile' like a shopping list to try to help them to identify what the **IDEAL** candidate should be like.

For example, someone selecting a marketing executive might decide that it is essential that the person should be of graduate level and desirable that they should have an upper second class honours degree. They may decide that it is essential that the person has very good interpersonal skills since they will be working with a variety of people, etc.

Some information is easy to establish such as exam grades, while other information, such as interpersonal skills, involves judgement and evaluation of your answers to questions.

Like many other decisions in life, recruitment decisions are often a compromise. The Person Profile is the recruiter's shopping list to help them to identify the ideal candidate.

When you are applying for jobs, work out 'what would be your ideal candidate for the job' if you were recruiting. What would you be looking for? Use the 'Person Profile' as a checklist.

Person Profile	Essential	Desirable
Physical make-up: height/build, appearance, health, speech, etc		
Attainments: education, qualifications, training, work achievements		
General intelligence: ability to sustain a logical argument, common sense, creativity		
Special aptitudes: numeracy, literacy, creativity, mechanical aptitude, dexterity, etc.		
Interests: Political, social, active outdoor, practical, intellectual, etc.		
Disposition: Interpersonal relationships, influence over others, industry, self-control, self-reliance, dependability, etc		
Circumstances: family and domestic, willingness to relocate, willingness to travel, etc.		
Motivation: Why this job – has the person got the 'can do' and 'will do'?		

Selection interviews

When you have spoken the word, it reigns over you. When it is unspoken you reign over it.

ARABIAN PROVERB

HOW YOU CAN PREPARE

The FBI say 'proper preparation and practice prevent a poor performance'. Prepare carefully and practice thoroughly for your interview. You will increase your confidence and your chances. Don't rely on charm and wit, there's too much at stake. Interviewers like well prepared candidates, who show a genuine interest.

Find out what you can about the job, the organisation, it's products or services. Get a copy of their annual report and product literature – getting a youngster to telephone the Public Relations department for a 'school project' is a good technique if you feel uncomfortable asking (although most people will view it positively if you request additional information). Research into the type of company; public, private, family owned, etc. – it's performance compared with competitors, etc.

If you can, talk to people who use the company's products; a friend of mine who applied for a job selling surgical devices spent a day in an operating theatre seeing the products in use. All he did was to ask the surgeon whether he could – yes, he got the job!

Get a copy of the job description if you can. If you can't, ask yourself why not? There may be a perfectly good reason or it may be that they haven't yet decided what your duties will be – a potential source of discontent for the future! (or, alternatively, because interviewees mirror a job description making it difficult to find out the actual interests/strengths, etc., of a candidate).

Re-read the advertisement, your application (you did remember to photocopy it before you posted it?) and your CV. Highlight what you can offer to match their requirements. Bear in mind that when companies recruit they rarely get a 'hand in glove' fit with a candidate who matches their requirements exactly. Your aim is to convince them that you are the best match.

Now is the time to cast modesty aside. It is almost certain that you will be asked something like, *'Tell me about yourself'* or *'What can you offer to our organisation?'*.

'Tell me about yourself'

Before the interview, write a short 'You' statement below, which answers these questions, making five or six positive statements (remember to include benefits) about yourself. Focus especially on your work skills. If you have completed the earlier activities this step should be straightforward.

Positive statement

1. I _____

2. I _____

3. I _____

4. I _____

5. I _____

6. I _____

Now practise saying it – yes, I know it feels uncomfortable but it is worth it, because it does work.

Practise the interview with a friend who is prepared to give you some feedback. Use a tape recorder or video camera (available on hire from many electrical stores and often cheap to rent midweek) to hear/see yourself as others do. Don't be despondent; we are all our own greatest critics and your accent isn't really that noticeable!

Are you up to date with developments in your field – scan the trade journals. You don't have to be a guru to be informed.

If you can, find out who will be interviewing you – think about what they might be looking for. This is particularly important if you are applying for a promotion or you already know the organisation well.

Decide an acceptable financial package – but let the interviewer raise it.

Plan your journey. There is virtually **no** excuse for being late for an interview. Allow extra time for rush-hour traffic, road works, and finding a parking space.

INTERVIEW DAY

Dress smartly in well-pressed, comfortable, clothes appropriate to the job/organisation. Get your hair trimmed. Do what you can to make yourself feel good – if you feel good inside, you'll present yourself well on the outside.

Arrive early so that you can prepare yourself. Admiral Horatio Nelson is reputed to have said, *'I owe my success in life to always being 15 minutes before my time'*. I can't vouch for the accuracy of the statement, but the principle is sound! Don't arrive more than fifteen minutes before the interview, however – wait outside. Some people see arriving much too early as poor time-management. They may be embarrassed to keep you waiting for a long time.

When you speak with receptionists and secretaries, remember they may be asked for their comments, as may the person who gave you an 'informal' tour of the site or offices before the interview.

Look around: could you work in these conditions, do people seem comfortable talking to each other, what is your impression of the culture? If you prefer a formal working environment where everyone is Mr or Ms etc., and you hear first names being used, the culture may not be right for you, and vice versa.

Leave the raincoat and umbrella in reception, so that you'll arrive at the interview uncluttered.

THE INTERVIEW

Smile and shake hands firmly, if the interviewer offers their hand.

Wait to be invited to sit down. If the wait seems too long ask, 'Where would you like me to sit?'

If you're offered a drink, accept it. Even if you only take one or two sips, it will be very useful if your throat starts to dry up.

Remember, you are well on the way to a job offer. The interviewer hopes you're the right person!

Take a few deep breaths, relax and be natural. This is your opportunity to show the interviewer that **you** are the person they're looking for.

Sit well back into your chair, in an upright but comfortable position. If you use your hands when talking, be aware of it and don't overdo it. Make friendly eye contact with the person asking questions. Don't stare. If you feel uncomfortable holding eye contact with people, look at the point of their forehead just above the nose – it works, honestly. If there is more than one interviewer, make sure you also involve them by addressing the next part of your answer to them. For panel interviews address the main body of an answer to the questioner, but then hold eye contact with other panel members in order to involve them. Only use the interviewer's first name if they invite you to.

Brevity is the essence of good communication. Pause briefly for a second to think before you speak. Don't ramble, wasting valuable time. The interviewer is more interested in the quality of your answer than the quantity! Don't waste too much time either talking about your early career; your **recent achievements** are usually far **more relevant**.

Listen actively to what is being asked or said – if you need to get a better understanding repeat or rephrase their question.

Be prepared for questions the interviewer knows you'll find difficult to answer, such as ones about a controversial subject. These are asked to see how you respond under pressure. Don't blurt out the answer; a short pause shows thoughtfulness.

Stress what it is about your skills and achievements that makes you the person for the job.

Introduce those five or six key 'YOU' points using benefit statements, (see Activity 23 'Selling Myself' on page 128). Help the interviewer to see how your skills and experience will benefit their organisation. It will be too late if you remember when you're half way home!

If the interviewer is your potential manager ask yourself whether you will be able to work with him or her.

Have a notepad and pen handy in your bag, pocket or briefcase to take any notes and answers to your questions at the end. This shows you have thought about the job. Questions you might like to use are shown near the end of this section.

Thank the interviewer and ask about the next step. This confirms your interest in the job.

Avoid:

- Smoking, even if the interviewer is.

- Showing references, job descriptions or samples of your work unless asked.

- Criticising employers and long stories about why you left jobs, particularly if you have a grievance with a previous employer.

- Talking about personal and domestic matters, unless asked.

- Getting on your soap box. What you do in your own time is of little concern to most employers, but few like activists or shop-floor politicians at work. Practise courteous answers to any likely questions.

- Raising salary/package. Let them know what you can do; this may well influence their view of what you are worth. Usually employers have a salary range in mind. If you ask about money too early they will give the lower figure. How many people do you know who have gone shopping to buy, say a hi-fi system with a price in mind of £500–£650 only to find that they buy one for £725? The same happens in recruitment.

- Name-dropping. It can backfire!

- Interrupting the interviewer in your enthusiasm to make all your points.

- Pretending you've got a better offer elsewhere to try to push them into a decision. But do let them know if you're being interviewed by other people – it can sometimes focus their minds! They don't want to miss you and don't give away too much information.

PREPARING FOR THEIR QUESTIONS

You can't know what is going to be asked but you can improve your chances by practising some common questions – ideally with a friend.

Start off with 'Tell me about yourself'. (Initial nervousness may cause you to say too much – don't).

If you're asked to talk about your career history and you've had a variety of jobs, don't dwell on your early career; the interview will have been scheduled for a set time and it is usually more important to talk about current/most recent responsibilities and achievements.

Now try answering some of the questions shown below. Paint the best image of yourself and show what you have to offer by talking about your skills and achievements.

Why did you leave ... ?

How are/were ... as employers?

What makes a 'good employer?

What have you been doing since you left ... ?

What did you enjoy doing at ... ?

What are your greatest strengths (weaknesses) as an employee?

What have been your best achievements?

What are the qualities needed in a good (job title)?

What qualities do you look for when recruiting subordinates?

If we offer you a job, what can you bring to our organisation?

What area of work do you feel least confident about?

What do your colleagues/manager see as your greatest weaknesses?

How would you describe your career progress to date?

What have you learned in your time with ... ?

What do you see yourself doing in 5/10/15 years?

Why did you become a (job title)?

How do you take direction?

How do you spend your holidays?

Have you ever been dismissed (disciplined)? Tell me about it.

How is your health?

How many days sick leave have you taken in the last two years?

How do you relax?

What do you know about our company?

Why do you want this job?

Why should we offer you this job?

Are you being interviewed for any other jobs?

Which do you want?

Some interviewers ask hypothetical questions along the lines of, 'How do you think you would react in ... situation?' Here you find yourself 'second guessing' them by saying how you would behave, in the way you think they want to hear! It can become quite an amusing game!

Other interviewers ask questions about what you have done in the past, since this is their best indicator of how you may perform in the future. They are looking for you to have handled situations in a positive way and for you to have learned from experience. Help them by:

- **Describing the situation and what had to be done**.
- **Explaining what you did**.
- **Describing the outcome in positive terms**.

Practise answering some of the questions below. They seem simple but are very searching!

Questions about your effort/initiative
Tell me about a project you initiated. What prompted you to begin it?

Give an example of when you did more than was required.

Given an example of when you worked the hardest and felt the greatest sense of achievement.

Planning and organising skills
What did you do to get ready for this interview?

How do you decide priorities in planning your time?

Give examples.

What are your objectives for this year? What are you doing to achieve them? How are you progressing?

Interpersonal skills
Describe a situation where you wished you'd acted differently with someone at work. What did you do? What happened?

Can you describe a situation where you found yourself dealing with someone whom you felt was over-sensitive. How did you handle it?

What unpopular decisions have you recently made? How did people respond? How did that make you feel?

Sales ability/persuasiveness
What are some of the best ideas you ever sold a superior/subordinate? What was your approach? Why did it succeed/fail?

Describe your most satisfying (disappointing) experience in attempting to gain support for an idea or proposal.

Decision making

What are the most important decisions you have made in the last year? How did you make them? What alternatives did you consider?

Describe an occasion when you involved others in your decision making. To what extent did you take notice of their input?

Leadership skills

What are some of the most difficult one-to-one meetings you have had with colleagues? Why where they difficult?

Have you been a member of a group where two of the members did not work well together? What did you do to get them to do so?

What do you do to set an example for others?

YOUR OWN QUESTIONS

Remember the recruitment interview is a two-way process. You may be making a choice about where you will spend the rest of your working life. Make the most of your opportunity to find out what you need to know and also to create a businesslike impression. **Start with questions which show an interest in the job**, not what the company can do for you.

Make a note of what you want to ask beforehand and if you need to, take brief notes of the answers. Examples of information you might like to gather (but not all at once!) could be:

The job

What will be your daily responsibilities/duties?

What is the level of the job within the company's grading structure?

To whom does the job report?

Is there a job description/what are the main priorities?

Reporting – up/down/sideways – are there any dotted line responsibilities?

What will be your budget availability?

What are relationships like with other departments?

What are the people like for whom you would be responsible? Are there any 'management' issues?

In what way is the company committed to your own training and development?

What are the opportunities for progress/career advancement?

What resources would you have available to help you achieve your goals?

The Company

What is the UK/total turnover?

Is there a statement on company philosophy/Mission Statement?

What is the company's profitability compared with competitors/budget?

How big is the workforce/turnover (of staff)?

What is the range of UK services/products?

What new products/services are under development?

What innovative ways are used to market their products/services?

Where will the company be in 5/10 years?

The practicalities (questions for when you are on the home straight!)
(when considering their offer keep the total package in mind.)

Medical – is it required?

Start date – how soon?

Pension – how is the scheme structured? Can you transfer in?

Salary review -based on what? How often? When will your first one be?

Car – allocation/running costs or charge?

Average salary increase last year/previous years (how is it reviewed)?

Holidays

Private healthcare – is it available? How much does it cost? Are spouse/family covered?

Insurance – what is the company scheme?

Bonus scheme – what is the structure?

Share options – are they available?

Salary – where does the figure they have offered fit in on their salary scales?

AFTERWARDS

Relax and congratulate yourself on having been as well prepared as you could be. Reflect on how it went and write down key points which could be important in a next interview.

You'll probably have to wait to hear their decision, but you can learn from the experience.

Were you happy with the way you handled yourself? Did you get across what you wanted to? Did you find out what you needed to know?

How many of 'YOU' points did you get across?

Was your behaviour positive, assertive, humble, tense, laid back, talkative, controlled, etc.?

If you've been put forward by a recruitment agency, call them as soon as you can to let them know how you got on and to confirm your interest in the job. They will almost certainly feed this straight back to the interviewer and it will be viewed positively. Otherwise, leave the ball in the court of the interviewer.

Don't become too despondent if you don't hear for a while – recruitment can sometimes take many weeks.

If, however they have promised to let you know, one way or the other, by a certain date and that day comes and goes, there is no harm done by telephoning to see how soon you are going to find out their decision.

Remember the interviewer is hoping that you are the right person for the job just as you are hoping to get the job. Do prepare and practise. It will be worth it.

Good luck!

Activity 30

Assessment centres

Diligence is the mother of good luck.
BENJAMIN FRANKLIN

Pioneered in the UK by the Armed Forces, Assessment Centres are now used by a number of organisations to select junior managers. They are very often re-labelled 'Development Centres' and used for internal selection purposes to identify fast-trackers and people with potential for promotion. For most candidates it's a once in a lifetime opportunity.

If you're invited to attend an Assessment Centre the following 'inside information' could be invaluable. See also the Activities on: Presentation Skills, Interview Skills and Tests and Evaluations. A form at the end of this Activity summarises the exercises at a typical Assessment Centre.

INSIDE INFORMATION

- Get as much sleep as you can beforehand. It's highly likely that, just as you're starting to relax, you'll be handed a mammoth task with a tight deadline to see how you respond under pressure.

- Keep your eyes and ears open and observe the performance of the other candidates. You may be asked to rate their performance. Be prepared to give a factual and analytical summary of their contribution.

- Don't be lulled into a false sense of security by thinking the assessors are off-duty, if you've been invited to join everyone for dinner the night before the Assessment Centre. They will probably be assessing your social competence over dinner, in the bar, over breakfast ....

- Even if you haven't been asked to prepare a presentation, brush up on your skills. There is a good chance that you'll be asked to prepare one at short-notice: Pre-select two topics: 'an improvement you've made at work' and an 'interesting angle on your hobby'.

- If you're invited to attend an Assessment Centre in a hotel, a few casual questions to the manager or receptionist may give you a good idea of what's in store.

- Try to think through the qualities the assessors will be looking for: leadership, interpersonal skills, ability to handle stress, verbal communication, written communication, flexibility, negotiation skills, problem solving, business skills, commercial acumen, decision taking, initiative and creativity. Clearly the weightings will change dependent on the job but commercial acumen, interpersonal skills and flexibility must be high on everyone's list.

- Don't try to suppress other candidates in an attempt to make the assessors notice only you. You will come across as overbearing and insensitive.

ASSESSMENT CENTRE EXERCISES

Assessment Centres are usually designed to include exercises which will measure you against the aspects of the job. For all of the exercises make sure you understand the Chairpersons instructions or the written brief. If you don't, **ask**!

Common exercises are:

In-tray exercises

You are given the 'in-tray' of a Senior Manager and have one hour to 'get through it' – otherwise you'll miss your plane! You'll be asked to write on each item what you would do with it, or write a reply to letters.

- Sort the whole thing first and prioritise every item: **A** (top priority), **B** and **C**. (They have probably 'buried' some important details near the bottom!)

- Start with the As and work your way through.

- Resignations and other 'people' issues are top priority As.

- Wherever you can, make a note that you would make a telephone call – the MD of one of my client companies, says that he writes no more than four memos per year.
- If you do write memos, write key messages and let your 'secretary' compose the letter.
- Familiarise yourself with the organisational structure of the company and the briefing instructions **before** you start.

Sales or negotiation role play

You are asked to sell a product or negotiate a deal.

- Ask 'probing' questions: How?, Why?, When?, Where?, What?, and Which?, are best.
- Listen to the answers! People who do badly in these exercises do so because they're too busy putting over their own viewpoint to understand what the other party wants.

Business simulation

You are split into small groups and over a series of rounds, compete with other groups to develop, manufacture, market and distribute products Great fun!

- Play to win!
- Invest in research for new products in the early rounds – products don't last forever.
- As you get results back at the end of each round analyse the performance of the competitors – you may be able to undercut them or market your product to a niche.

Group discussion (interactive skills)

You are given a problem to solve as a group. Common problems are simulations where your group have been stranded at sea, in the desert or on the moon. (See page 164 for an example of an Assessor's form.)

- If you're 'stranded' in the desert or on the ocean, being detected is the first priority, followed by food – don't move away to try to save yourself; search parties look for your last location!
- Formulate your own ideas quickly and sell them convincingly to the group.
- Suggest that the group needs a structure and timetable to work to; and propose one.
- Don't steamroller other people's ideas, listen attentively.

- If someone isn't contributing, draw them into the group by asking for their ideas.
- Five minutes before the end suggest that you need to summarise your decision and take control of whatever needs to be done.

MAKE THE MOST OF THE OPPORTUNITY

An Assessment Centre is a tremendous opportunity for you to show what you can do. Prepare yourself well and enjoy it. In summary, **be positive, be prepared to play the game** and project an image of your real self.

INTERACTIVE SKILLS ASSESSMENT

Candidate name _____ Assessor _____

Behaviour	Quality/Quantity of Contribution	Rating
Giving Information		
Seeking Information		
Supporting Others		
Disagreeing with Others		
Persuading Others		
Controlling Others		
Other Contributions		

COMMENTS

STANDARDS

5   Much more than acceptable (significantly above criteria required for successful job performance).

4   More than acceptable (generally exceeds criteria relative to quality and quantity of behaviour required).

3   Acceptable (meets criteria relative to quality and quantity of behaviour required).

2   Less than acceptable (generally does not meet criteria relative to quality and quantity of behaviour required).

1   Much less than acceptable (significantly below criteria required for successful job performance).

Overall rating _____

SELECTION PANEL ASSESSMENT FORM: POSITION _____

Chairperson _____

Other panel members _____

_____

_____

Interview date: _____

EXERCISE

Candidate	Leaderless Group Discussion	In-Tray Exercise	Presentation	Marketing Plan	1:1 Negotiation	Interpersonal /Social Skills	Interview No. 1	Interview No. 2	Assessment
1.									
2.									
3.									
4.									
5.									
6.									

Panel Recommendation: _____

Making a presentation

It usually takes me more than three weeks to prepare a good impromptu speech.

MARK TWAIN

To assess your self-confidence, ability to communicate and ability to handle a mini-project, some organisations may ask you to make a short presentation either to a group of managers or, for very senior positions, to the Board of Directors. Others incorporate a presentation into their assessment centre exercises.

The subject can vary from debating the pros and cons of the Channel Tunnel through to presenting a mini-marketing plan for one of the company's products or they may even leave the choice of subject to you. If this happens do not pick 'Where I Took My Holiday' or 'My Hobby'. Do choose a business-related subject that you know something about. The time you are given to prepare can vary from 30 minutes to many days.

If you are asked to give a presentation do take it seriously – management time is very valuable and if the company have gathered an audience to listen to you, then you can be sure that they will be taking it seriously.

Unless you are a natural or are well experienced, you will probably be nervous. This is a good thing. If you didn't have at least some degree of anxiety then you probably aren't taking the exercise seriously.

The keys to an effective presentation are **preparation**, **planning** and **practice.**

PREPARE THE CONTENT

Most people find knowing where to begin is the most difficult step. If you are one of these people I can guarantee the following steps will help you present confidently.

Ask yourself – 'What do I want the audience to **learn** from my presentation?'

Write this objective in the middle of a blank page. Now let your mind 'free-wheel' to produce a mind-map of ideas. The mind-map on page 165 is the one I drew when I started to plan this Activity, which was originally published as an article called 'How to Give a Presentation and Live to Tell the Tale'.

You'll find that you have far too many things to say, so the next step is to edit and give the presentation some structure.

MIND-MAP

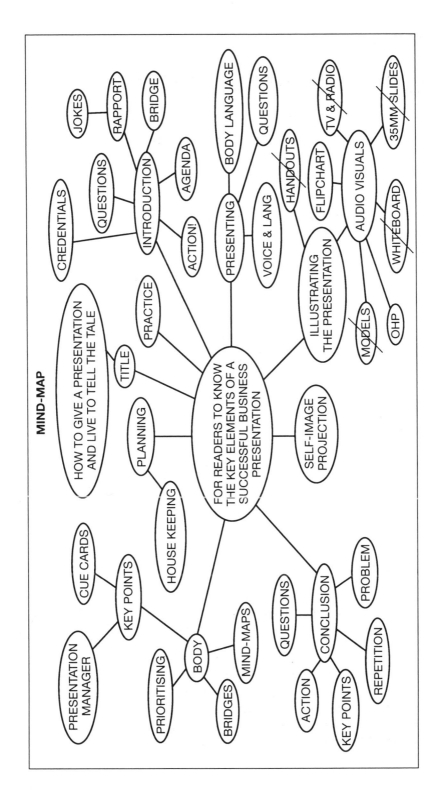

Now choose the most important point which you want to communicate. Write it in on The Presentation Planner (there is a blank copy at the end of this Activity) as Key Point No 1. Now add the others in descending order of priority.

Yes, I know that the natural tendency is to save the best 'til last, but remember that people are most attentive at the start.

Now develop your content by putting the information from your mind-map into your Key Points. Remember, only information which is relevant to achieving your objectives is allowed. Limit your Key Points to a maximum of five. Three is even better. Think about the presenters you admire – are they the ones who put over powerful and succinct argument or are they the people who waffle and constantly overrun?

You have now developed the main body of your presentation. But before we move on, decide how you will link or bridge, from one point to the next. A phrase like, 'Now let us look at the introduction' lets the listeners know you've finished one topic and gives a signpost of what's next.

Other useful bridges are: enumerating – 'First ..., Second ..., etc.' when you've stated that you have a specific number of points to cover; 'On the contrary' or 'On the other hand' when you're weighing pros and cons; or simply, 'Next ...'. To avoid sounding hackneyed, use a different bridge to move from each of your key points. Now write them on your Presentation Planner.

Your introduction

You get one opportunity to make a first impression. So how do you create that positive impression from the start?

The first step is to establish empathy by building a bridge to as many audience members as you can. If you can, speak informally to each person before you begin.

When you stand to address the group, reinforce the bridge by saying 'How much you've been looking forward to meeting them' ... and pay some compliment to their office, factory, etc.

If you're considering starting with a joke, my advice is don't. You never know whom you may offend and alienate. This isn't to say you shouldn't be warm, friendly and charming. But as well as having the potential to offend, actors will tell you that comedy is the most difficult of all stage techniques to master.

Now say what you're going to talk about, seen from their viewpoint.

But why should they listen to **you**? You should say a few words here about why you are qualified to speak on this topic, what you have done to research the subject, what is your background in this field, etc. Two or three sentences establish your credibility.

Now for the agenda. Give the audience a 'map' of what you'll be talking about. The agenda is a list of the Key Points which make up the body of the presentation.

'As we go through the presentation please feel free to ask questions, if I haven't explained anything clearly; although we do have a few moments at the end for questions.' Let's face it, telling people to save their questions until the end rarely works. So why not prepare for it? Doing it this way also signals to the audience that you're confident of what your talking about.

Next, state quite clearly what you want **them** to do as a result of listening to you; the Action Request. 'When I've finished speaking I hope you will see that the strategy I am advocating will help to re-position (product) in the market-place.'

And finally your bridge. How do you link to the first Key Point in the body? Now write each of these into your Presentation Planner.

In conclusion

Your conclusion should be short and to the point, but not rushed. You want to encapsulate your presentation into a package that they can take away with them.

Remind them of the problem or opportunity. Restate your Key Points and crystalise the message. State your Request Action – what you want them to do?

This structure for your presentation ensures that your Key Points are repeated at least three times and repetition is a very powerful persuader. Just watch commercial television to see how often advertisements are repeated, if you need convicing.

Now write your conclusion on your Presentation Planner.

To summarise, with apologies to whoever said it first, your structure will allow you to: 'Tell them what you're going to tell them, then tell them and then tell them what you've told them'.

PLAN YOUR RESOURCES

Now you have decided what you are going to say, you can concentrate on how you say it.

Transfer your introduction, Key Points (in the correct order) and conclusion on to postcards, using single words to act as stab points. Do not write a script, it will make your voice become dull and lifeless.

Now punch a hole into the top right hand corner or each card and loosely tie them together with a piece of string. This way your presentation will keep in the correct order, even if you drop the cards. (When you deliver your presentation, don't be afraid to glance at your cue cards. A momentary pause is far more acceptable than waffle or a deathly hush, because you can't think what to say next.)

Visual aids are useful in your presentation since they can convey information – try describing the layout of a printed circuit board or how to fold a napkin in words! Your visual aids reinforce what you are saying by focusing the audience's attention.

The most convenient visual aids to use are the flipcharts or overhead transparencies. Either are available at good commercial stationers.

The flipchart can be very useful for developing diagrams in front of your audience – write the words/draw the diagram in advance in pencil on the flipchart sheet. The audience will not be able to see the fine lines and you will be confident that the layout will be correct when you start to build up the chart in front of your audience, using marker pens. Ensure that you have at least two pens available and check that they both work before the presentation.

Overhead transparencies are a convenient way for producing visual aids. You can either photocopy diagrams or words directly on to the transparency or you can use special pens (I prefer the permanent kind since they do not smudge). Use only the dark colours – pretty as the yellows and oranges are, they can't be read!

Whichever visual aids you use, follow the basic principles of keeping them as simple as possible. Use large letters and single words as stab points so that they can be read easily. Do not write complete sentences. Remember a picture is worth a thousand words. As a general rule allow 45 seconds to 1 minute per transparency when planning your time.

PRACTISE

Rehearse your presentation once or twice so that you know what you are going to say and how you are going to say it. Use a friend as a timekeeper to give you constructive feedback.

PREPARATION AND PRESENTATION

Get a good night's sleep and no matter how nervous you are, avoid alcohol or stimulants!

Here are a few do's and don'ts for you to bear in mind when presenting:

Do	Don't
Use global vision to include everyone	Use non-words, like ums and errs
Hold eye contact with people	Jingle coins/keys in pockets
Check focus beforehand	Clean out/scratch orifices
Check power beforehand	Talk to the floor, the screen or one main audience member
Set up the room beforehand	Read visuals word for word
Use clear, concise visuals	Joke – you don't know whom you might offend
Vary tone and speed of your voice	Mumble
Stand relatively stationary	Apologise for what you're going to say
Have spare pens/transparencies	Dress outrageously
Keep to time	Smoke – even if audience members do
Use simple language	Remove your jacket
End on a positive note	Use a pointer – they're too easy to play with

ANSWERING QUESTIONS

Generally speaking the assessors are aware of your time pressures and so will save questions until the end.

If you're asked a question that you can't answer then be honest – you'll gain more credibility from this than from half-baked waffle. You can in fact turn your lack of knowledge to your advantage by saying to the questioner. 'That's an interesting point which I haven't been asked before. I'm afraid I don't have an answer for you right now, but I will find out and get back to you'. This technique flatters the questioner's ego and demonstrates your integrity.

WHAT ARE THE ASSESSORS LOOKING FOR?

Unless you've applied for a job as a television presenter or a similar position which involves speaking to groups on a regular basis, it is unlikely that the assessors will be looking for outstanding skills.

The assessors will be looking for you to communicate your message effectively, for you to project yourself confidently and for you to know what you are talking about. Remember, even the most experienced presenters get nervous – use the adrenaline to help you to excel!

The form on the next page is an example of what may be used to assess your presentation.

ASSESSMENT CENTRE – PRESENTATION SCORE SHEET

Ten minute presentation with five minutes' questions and answers from Assesors.

Candidate: _____ **Assessor:** _____

Criteria	Comments	Rating
Content		
Delivery (voice/posture)		
Pace		
Use of Visuals		
Audience Contact		
Handling Questions		
Other Comments		

STANDARDS

5   Much more than acceptable (significantly above criteria required for successful job performance).

4   More than acceptable (generally exceeds criteria relative to quality and quantity of behaviour required).

3   Acceptable (meets criteria relative to quality and quantity of behaviour required).

2   Less than acceptable (generally does not meet criteria relative to quality and quantity of behaviour required).

1   Much less than acceptable (significantly below criteria required for successful job performance).

Overall rating _____

PRESENTATION PLANNER

Introduction	Main body	Conclusion
Rapport Statement	Key Point 1	Remind them of the Problem/Opportunity
Presentation Subject (their viewpoint)	Bridge	
Your Credentials	Key Point 2	Restate the Key Points and crystallise the message
Agenda	Bridge	
Question Request	Key Point 3	
	Bridge	
Action Request	Key Point 4	Request Action
	Bridge	
Bridge	Key Point 5	
	Bridge	

Copyright waiver: this page may be photocopied by purchasers of the book (it is advisable to enlarge to A3 or A4).

Tests and evaluations

It is hard to fail, but it is worse never to have tried to succeed. In this life we get nothing save by effort.

THEODORE ROOSEVELT

Some organisations use tests and evaluations in their selection process.

Before inviting people to interview, the recruiter identifies personality traits, skills and knowledge which would be held by the ideal candidate. During the selection process candidates are asked to complete 'tests' to evaluate whether they possess these qualities.

The extent of the testing can vary from a short five-minute form-filling exercise through to a whole day, involving a battery of tests and evaluations and an interview with a psychologist.

I cannot stress too strongly that there is no need to get anxious about the tests! I know it's easy for me to say that ... I'm not the one who has been invited to interview! Seriously, the tests will not reveal that really you're an alien from Mars (you aren't are you?) or that you're not really a person ... you're a slug who lives in an aquarium and just for today you've transformed yourself into a person! Take them in your stride do your best and be honest.

PERSONALITY QUESTIONNAIRES

As their name implies the questionnaires aim to gain an insight into your personality. I do not like the use of the word 'test' when related to personality evaluations. 'Test' implies 'right and wrong' and in personality evaluations there are no right and wrong answers – we are all different.

Usually there is no time limit for a personality questionnaire, but you are advised not to over-analyse your reply and to move quickly from question to question. Don't answer questions as you **think** you should. Be honest to yourself, otherwise you're defeating the object. Also, some personality questionnaires have an 'in-built' evaluation which checks to see how (honest) consistent your answers have been.

The most commonly used personality questionnaires are the Myers-Briggs Type Inventory (MBTI), this claims to be the most widely used one in the world, the Saville and Holdsworth; Occupational Personality Quotient (S.H.L., O.P.Q.), The Sixteen Personality Factors (16PF); and one by Thomas International. There are many others.

SKILLS AND APTITUDE TESTS

Unlike personality questionnaires, skill and aptitude tests **are** designed to test you against standards.

Typing tests are used to evaluate your keyboard skills and typing accuracy. Tests of manual dexterity, such as rebuilding a broken-down model, test your 'motor skills'.

Others represent an intellectual challenge such as numerical, verbal and abstract reasoning tests!

- **Numerical** – Identifies the ability to pick out and manipulate key information from tables, graphs and semi-technical reports.

- **Verbal** – Identifies the ability to pick out information from reports and then make objective decisions based on the information in the text.

- **Abstract** – Tests the ability to think flexibly. The test measures the ability to recognise order in the midst of apparent chaos, to focus on certain aspects of a task and to ignore irrelevant detail.

Your score in the tests will be compared against 'norm' tables to see how you have performed, compared with previous groups of people who have taken the test.

On the following pages I have reprinted two 'Test Taker's Guides'.

The '**General Ability Tests**' are used for the selection of staff below graduate level and for the identification of potential for supervisory and junior management posts, regardless of previous experience or education.

The '**Graduate and Managerial Assessment**' tests are used in recruiting at graduate and managerial level.

I am grateful to ASE, of Windsor for their permission to reproduce the 'Test-Taker's Guides'.

TEAM TYPE QUESTIONNAIRES

Work by Dr Meredith Belbin has shown that groups are most productive when there is a good mixture of people who can contribute various skills to the team. The 'Team Type' questionnaire is used to gauge how well you will fit into the team.

None of the team types is the 'best' type to be – productive teams have a mix of the different types.

The following summary describes the various Team Types.

- **Plant**: Creative, imaginative, unorthodox. Solves difficult problems. Weak in communicating with and managing ordinary people.

- **Resource investigator**: Extrovert, enthusiastic, communicative. Explores opportunities. Develops contacts. Loses interest once initial enthusiasm has passed.

- **Chairperson/co-ordinator**: Mature, confident and trusting. A good chairperson. Clarifies goals, promotes decision-making. Not necessarily the most clever or creative member of a group.

- **Shaper**: Dynamic, outgoing, highly strung. Challenges, pressurises, finds ways round obstacles. Prone to provocation and short-lived bursts of temper.

- **Monitor evaluator**: Sober, strategic and discerning. Sees all options. Judges accurately. Lacks drive and ability to inspire others.

- **Teamworker**: Social, mild, perceptive and accommodating. Listens, builds, averts friction. Indecisive in crunch situations.

- **Company worker/implementer**: Disciplined, reliable, conservative and efficient. Turns ideas into practical actions. Somewhat inflexible, slow to respond to new possibilities.

- **Completer**: Painstaking, conscientious, anxious. Searches out errors and omissions. Delivers on time. Inclined to worry unduly. Reluctant to delegate.

- **Expert/specialist**: Single-minded, self-starting, dedicated. Provides knowledge or technical skills in rare supply. Contributes only on a narrow front.

To find out your own 'Team Type' you'll need Dr Belbin's book, *Management Teams: Why They Succeed or Fail*, which contains the questionnaire (see Appendix for details).

DRUG AND ALCOHOL TESTING

Concerned with the effect that alcohol and drug abuse has on productivity, some employers require a urine sample which is tested for drugs and alcohol. These tests are **very** rare in the UK but common in the USA, so they are more likely if you're applying to the UK affiliate of a large US company.

GRAPHOANALYSIS (HANDWRITING ANALYSIS)

You won't even be aware that it's being carried out! Graphoanalysis claims to be able to interpret the personality of a person from their handwriting. It is widely used, I understand, in continental Europe, particularly in France, but is not very widely used in the UK, although one UK Consultancy offering this service has over 100 clients.

To end on a positive note! A good employer will always give you feedback from these tests, whether you get offered the job or not – but usually only if you ask!

Profile instruments, evaluations, assessments, or whatever you wish to call them, are not free: they cost the recruiting organisation both time and money. If they're being used, they're serious about your application.

They are another way for you to show you're the right person for the job!

☺ **My Jobsearching Do's** ☺

_____
_____
_____
_____

☹ **My Jobsearching Don'ts** ☹

_____
_____
_____
_____

Use these notepads to summarise your learning points as you complete activities in *I can do that!*

What if I didn't get the job I wanted?

Every noble work is at first impossible.

THOMAS CARLYLE

You were down to a shortlist of two. People were making such positive noises about how you would fit into the organisation and then a letter this morning ... 'Thank you for attending interview ... I am sorry to inform you that ...' and the world falls away from under your feet. I commiserate with you – they have obviously picked the wrong person.

CAN YOU TURN THE SITUATION TO ADVANTAGE?

- Write to them quickly to say how disappointed you were and how impressed you had been with their company. Say that if any other vacancies arise in the near future you would like to be considered. Alternatively telephone them to say the same things and to ask for some feedback on why you didn't get the job – most employers will give you some constructive critique and you never know, you *may* be able to re-open discussions; it *can* work. See Activity 27.
- Follow up your letter with a phone call.
- What have you learned from the process? It may be not to put all of your eggs in one basket or to conduct yourself differently at recruitment interviews.

Make a few notes below.

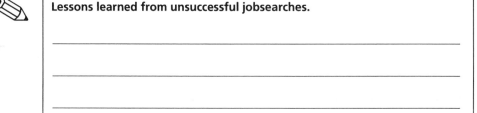

Lessons learned from unsuccessful jobsearches.

_____

_____

_____

WHAT DO I DO WHEN I HAVE ARRIVED?

...uuve/Acc...
...strator Advertising...
...aftEngineer AirlinePilot A...
...mal TechnicianAnthropologis...
...okseller AntiqueDealer Archaeo.
...rchitect Archiver ArtDealer Astron
...uctioneer BalletDancer Banker Barr
Biochemist Botanist Bookseller Broad
Broker Builder Careers Advisor Cart...
Cardiologist Chemical Engineer Chir
...lerkCoastguard Community Worke...
...cretaryComputerEngineerConduct...
...igner Dentist Development Engin...
...tor Dispensing Optician Doctor
...ainer Draughtsman Driving...
...ist Economist Editor Educat...
...cal Engineer Electronic Engin...
...ainer Environmental Heal...
...iomist Estate Agent E...
...ort Agent Fabric Desig...
...rm Manager Fashion Ph...
...ilmDirector Financial Ma...
...ish Farmer Flight Controller F...
...nologist Footwear Manufactur...
...Office Executive Forensic Scientist...
...Forwarder Game Keeper Geneticist G...

...urance...
...urographicSurvey...
...ormationScientistInsura...
...terior Designer International...
...vellery Designer Journalist Land...
...awyerLegal Accountant Librarian...
...ousekeeperLoss Adjuster Magazine...
...Management Accountant Marine Eng...
...arketing Manager Media Planner M...
...nysicist Merchant Banker Metallurgi...
...Microbiologist Missionary Model Mu...
...Naval Architect Neurophysiologist N...
...ngineer Nurse Occupational Thera...
...ce Manager Optician Packagin...
...ter Patent Agent Personnel M...
...macist Physicist Pianist Poli...
...ter Probation Officer Psychia...
...blic Administrator Publis...
...reational Manager R...
...ager School Inspector...
...erson Silversmith Socio...
...oker Surveyor Systems A...
...Textile Designer Theatre Man...
...g Standards Officer Travel Agen...
...erwriter Veterinary Surgeon Wate...
...outh Worker Zoo Keeper Zoologist Z

Introduction to Phase IV

Experience shows us that success is due less to ability than to zeal. The winner is the one who gives themself to their work; body and soul.
CHARLES BUXTON

Congratulate yourself!

CELEBRATE

and don't forget to say thank you to those who have helped you on your way.

Well done.

Saying goodbye to my previous employer

Don't flatter yourself that friendship authorises you to say disagreeable things to your intimates. The nearer you come into relation with a person, the more necessary do tact and courtesy become.

OLIVER WENDELL HOLMES

THE PRACTICAL ASPECTS

Make sure you know the name of the pension fund administrator so that you can keep them updated of changes of address and whether you want to change Pension Schemes.

THE PERSONAL ASPECTS

If you're leaving on bad terms **DON'T, DON'T, DON'T** be rude, abusive or disrespectful to your ex-employer. **No matter how much venom there is on the inside; control it and keep it there**.

Now I'm not offering this advice in the interests of your ex-employers, but in yours. No matter how bitter you are feeling, try to **leave on amicable terms**. The reason for this is that **most** new employers will want a reference from your past employer. Even if you don't need it immediately for a new job, you might need it in a year or two.

You'll do neither your own self-esteem, nor your future job prospects, any good if you lose your temper and are abusive to your boss. If you want to vent your anger try writing a letter to your ex-boss. Don't hold anything back. Now tear it up and throw it in the waste bin!

Try to 'negotiate' the wording of your reference before you leave so that it can be placed on your Personnel File. People move on and it may be that, only a few months after you have left an organisation, a Personnel Officer whom you have never met, will complete a 'Company Reference' for you, based on the contents of your Personnel File.

Accepting the new job

What we obtain too cheap, we esteem too lightly; it is dearness only that gives everything its value.

THOMAS PAINE

'Yippee – I've filled the vacancy!'   *'Yippee – I got the job.'*

'Yipee I got the new job! (candidate's view) 'Yippee I've filled the vacancy! (employer's view) 'I think it's what's called a win-win scenario by negotiators. Both parties have benefited.

As soon as your potential employer starts to display buying signals you should be ready to begin the negotiation around your earnings package.

I've said earlier that you should let the employer raise salary first, but you should also realise that they will not normally make their best offer up-front.

NEGOTIATING THE BEST PACKAGE

In some occupations, salaries are fixed according to seniority and years of service. In others there is a good deal of flexibility around certain variables.

Remember, **when you have accepted an offer, you have accepted it,**

You'll create a bad impression if you accept the job and then go back two days later, trying to re-negotiate the terms of the contract.

So before you enter the negotiating arena it's worth working out what is the minimum package you are prepared to accept and what you would like to get.

Realistically, there will be some aspects of the package which will be fixed, e.g., holidays which will be written in policies and procedures.

KNOWLEDGE IS POWER

The following page is taken from a real Salary Survey,* with the job title removed for confidentiality. As you will see, there are large differences between the minimum and maximum salaries and values of company cars. The lowest paid job pays £17,000 p.a. with no company car whilst the best job pays almost £32,000 p.a. with a £15,000 company car. A huge difference, yet these people hold the same job title, in different organisations.

While you are in the discussing phase, i.e., before anything is committed to paper, ask:

1. Where does the salary fit into their own internal salary scales?
2. Where does the salary fit in, on the salary surveys, for a person with similar experience doing a similar job? Company policy may be that they pay a 'lower quartile' salary (in other words 75 per cent of people doing a similar job earn more) to a new starter, with the objective of shifting you to the upper quartile within three years. Try to convince them that your skills and experience warrant being started higher up the scale.

Remember you probably won't be able to re-negotiate a package once you have accepted it so tread carefully.
An extra £500 per year over a career is an awful lot of money!

*Salary Survey example kindly supplied by Alan Jones & Associates.

An example of a page from a salary survey

A SURVEY GROUP

JOB 88: CONFIDENTIAL

ALAN JONES & ASSOCIATES   A.J

JOB SALARY DETAILS

TOTAL NUMBER OF JOBHOLDERS : 70
NO. OF COMPANIES REPORTING : 19

COMPANY CODE(L)	JOB HLDRS	MOD	RATE MNTH	+++++SALARY RANGE+++++ MINIMUM	CONTROL	MAXIMUM	++++++ACTUAL AVERAGE+++++++ BASIC	BonusV	BonusF	TOTAL	COMPA RATIO	++++++ACTUAL MEDIAN+++++++ BASIC	BonusV	BonusF	TOTAL	COMPA RATIO	CAR VALUE
01 (2)	1	:	5	25142	31428	37713	31250		601	31851	99	31250		601	31851	99	15184
28 (3)	2	=	7	19425	26574	33900	26261	4280	447	27988	88	26261	4280	447	27988	88	13655
10 (3)	1	=	11	24549	30066	36814	26586		1108	27694	88	26586		1108	27694	88	17050
18 (3)	8	=	7	23606	29508	35410	26000			26000	88	26000			26000	88	14000
22 (3)	2	=	11	19945	24170	29385	23599	1244		25719	101	24365	1200		25316	95	13500
07 (3)	1	=	11	23300	29124	34949	24882	726	991	25316	81	24882	726	991	25316	81	13300
19 (4)	6	=	3	20182	25227	30272	24882		662	24882	99	24570		662	24570	97	
02 (4)	4	=	8	22300	23100	33440	23100	808		24570	100	23100	808		23885	100	17040
16 (4)	4	=	11	19731	27870	29596	23440	880		24320	84	23238	347		23657	83	15300
17 (4)	4	=	1	21122	24664	31785	21704	1953		23657	88	21704	1953		23845	88	11500
11 (4)	12	=	1	20097	26454	30146	21763	1750		23513	88	22000	1845		23845	83	14354
21 (5)	1	=	1	16688	20859	25030	22713			22713	90	22250			22250	89	13634
14 (4)	2	=	1	17379	21724	26342	20650	567		21627	93	20650	567		21627	93	
23 (4)	7	=	10	18000	19875	26069	21250	810		21460	94	21250	810		21460	94	15000
29 (4)	6	=	8	18640	22840	22000	19875			21250	98	19875			21250	98	
05 (4)	4	=	0	18300	19900	27035	18900	900		19800	83	19125	695		19875	100	12700
20 (4)	6	=					18633			18633	94	18300			18300	84	
12 (4)	3	=	0	12819	14594	16282	17000			17000	116	17000			17000	116	11389

	++SALARY RANGE++ ++CONTROL++ UNWTD	WTD	++++++ACTUAL AVERAGE++++++ ++BASIC++ UNWTD	WTD	+++TOTAL++ UNWTD	WTD	++++++ACTUAL MEDIAN++++++ ++BASIC++ UNWTD	WTD	+++TOTAL++ UNWTD	WTD	CAR VALUE UNWTD	WTD
MAXIMUM	31428	31428	31250	31250	31851	31851	31250	31250	31851	31851	17050	17050
UPPER QUARTILE	27222	25227	24037	23440	25517	24882	23430	23075	24200	24943	15138	15138
MEDIAN	24664	24417	22713	21974	23657	22713	22250	21687	22250	23657	13827	13827
AVERAGE	24476	23947	22557	21974	23572	22732	22424	21355	22379	23403	14093	14093
LOWER QUARTILE	21838	21952	20262	19875	21355	19875	20262	19875	19875	21355	13125	13125
MINIMUM	14594	14594	17000	17000	17000	17000	17000	17000	17000	17000	11389	11389

Starting my new job

Ah, but a man's reach should exceed his grasp, Or what's heaven for?.
ROBERT BROWNING

Congratulations. What you have reached for, has come within your grasp! Everything we have been working on together has come to fruition.

If I can offer some final advice, don't hide this book away in a cupboard and forget about it – come back to it now and again to see how well you are progressing against your goals.

And don't forget what we have been saying all along about transferable skills – in your jobsearch you have been developing a wide variety of transferable skills: Active Listening, Interpersonal Communication and Networking to name just three. Transfer them with you into your new job – don't leave them in the cupboard.

Good Luck. I wish you every success in your new job.

When you win ... nothing hurts
JOE NAMETH, NEW YORK JETS

Appendix

This contains:

- **Useful addresses and telephone numbers** (These cover jobsearching and career and life planning, as well as other aspects of family life)
- **Contacts for further information**
- **Additional Reading**

Advice can often be in short supply when you're jobsearching.

This appendix has been developed to help in your jobsearching and career and life planning. You will also find a wealth of addresses and telephone numbers which you may never use ... but if you do need them, you know where to look.

Request for help: If you have published a book or a leaflet, or are involved with a voluntary body, which should be brought to the attention of jobsearchers, please write to me;

Malcolm Hornby, c/o Pitman Publishing, 128 Long Acre, London, WC2E 9AN.

ADVICE (GENERAL)

Benefits Agency. Quarry House, Quarry Hill, Leeds LS2 7UA. DSS Freeline Social Security: 0800 666555. Responsible for paying Social Security benefits. The addresses and general numbers of the 500 local offices are in the telephone directory.

Citizens Advice Bureaux. (see local telephone directory) Provides free, confidential and impartial information and advice on every subject to everybody, regardless of race, gender, sexuality or disability.

Crossroads Care Attendant Schemes Ltd. 10 Regent Place, Rugby, Warks CV21 2PN. Tel: 0788 573653. Offers respite care to enable carers to take a break from looking after an ill or disabled relative at home.

Law Centres Federation. Duchess House, 18-19 Warren Street, London W1P 5DB. Tel: 071-387 8570. Aim to promote and support the 55 Law Centres located throughout the UK. Centres provide independent free legal advice and representation to those living in the area.

Lesbian and Gay Switchboard. BM Switchboard, London WC1N 3XX. Helpline: 071-837 7324. LLGS is run by lesbian and gay volunteers offering confidential advice, information and referrals to lesbians and gays, their friends and families.

Salvation Army. 101 Queen Victoria Street, London EC4P 4EP. Tel: 071-236 5222. Second only to the government as a provider of social services in the UK. Provides practical and spiritual support to help improve the quality of family life.

The Samaritans. Head office: 10 The Grove, Slough SL1 1QP. Tel: 0753 532713 (local Helpline numbers in phone directory). Provide confidential support to suicidal and despairing people, 24 hours a day, 7 days a week.

Shelter. 88 Old Street, London EC1V 9HU. Tel: 071-253 0202. Shelter, The National Campaign for Homeless People, combines practical help through a national network of 29 housing advice centres. Provides emergency shelter in London.

Shelter Scotland. Head office: 8 Hampton Terrace, Edinburgh EH12 5JD. Tel: 031-313 1550. Works to relieve poverty and distress among homeless people, campaigns for provision of housing and runs charity shops.

Victim Support (National Association of Victim Support Schemes). Cranmer House, 39 Brixton Road, London SW9 6DZ. Tel: 071-735 9166. Trained volunteers based in local schemes offer free confidential support and advice.

Victim Support Scotland. 14 Frederick Street, Edinburgh EH2 2HB. Tel: 031-225 7779. Provides a listening ear to victims of crime and practical help and advice with house security; claims to Criminal Injuries Compensation Board; accompany victims to court.

Women's Aid Federation England. PO Box 391, Bristol BS99 7WS. Tel: 0272 633494. Provide emergency and temporary accommodation, advice, information and support services to abused women and children.

Scottish Women's Aid. 12 Torphichen Street, Edinburgh EH13 8JQ. Helpline: 031-221 0401. Provide information, support and temporary refuge for abused women and their children.

Women Against Rape: King's Cross Women's Centre, 71 Tonbridge Street, London WC1H 9DZ. Tel: 071-837 7509. Offers counselling, legal advice and support for women and girls who have been raped/sexually assaulted.

Working Mothers/Parents at Work. 77 Holloway Road, London N7 8JZ. Helpline: 071-700-5771. A self-help organisation for working mothers and their children. Through a network of local groups they provide an informal support system.

BIRTHS

British Pregnancy Advisory Service. Austy Manor, Wooton Wawen, Solihull, West Midlands B95 6BX. Tel: 0564 793225. Offers support and counselling.

Family Planning Association. 27-35 Mortimer Street, London W1N 7RJ. Tel: 071-636 7866. Provide advice and resources through their helpline and a range of publications.

Issue (The National Fertility Association Ltd). 509 Aldridge Road, Great Barr, Birmingham B44 8NA. Tel: 021-344 4414. Issue has qualified consultants and volunteers.

Life. Life House, 1A Newbold Terrace, Leamington Spa, Warwicks CV32 4AE. Helpline: 0926 311511. National charity specialising in pregnancy and abortion counselling, counselling after abortion, pre- and post-birth accommodation, and an education service for schools.

Lifeline Pregnancy Care. Cae Bach, 4 Pant y Wennol Bodafon, Llandudno, Gwynedd LL30 3DS. Tel: 0492 543741. Provide support, practical help and professional, non-directional counselling to women with unplanned pregnancies as well as post-abortion counselling.

Meet-a-Mum Association (MAMA) 14 Illis Road, Croydon, Surrey CR0 2XX. Helpline: 081-656 7318. Aims to put mothers in touch with other mothers living nearby for friendship and support. Services include advice on postnatal depression.

Miscarriage Association. (Acknowledging Pregnancy Loss) Head Office: c/o Clayton Hospital, Northgate, Wakefield, West Yorkshire WF1 3JS. Tel: 0924 200799. Provides support and information for those suffering the distress of baby loss through miscarriage.

National Childbirth Trust. Alexandra House, Oldham Terrace, London W3 6HN. Tel: 081-992 8637. Offers information and support in pregnancy, childbirth and early parenthood.

Tamba (Twins and Multiple Births Association). PO Box 30, Little Sutton, South Wirral L66 1TH. Tel: 051-348 0020 (Helpline: 0732 868000). Supports families with twins, triplets or more.

Well Being. 27 Sussex Place, Regents Park, London NW1 4SP. Tel: 071-262 5337. Well Being is the charity that funds medical research for the better health of women and babies in hospitals and universities all over Britain.

CAREER OPTIONS

Visit the reference section of your local library.

A – Z of Careers and Jobs, Diane Burston, London, Kogan Page.

'*Careers In*' series, London, Kogan Page. (30 titles)

'*CODOT*' (Classification of Occupations and Directory of Occupational Titles), Norwich, HMSO

Occupations, Careers and Occupational Information Centre, Sheffield. Published annually, covering opportunities in the professions, industry, commerce and the public service.

Offbeat Careers, 60 Ways to avoid Becoming an Accountant, Vivien Donald, London, Kogan Page.

'*Running your Own*' series, Kogan Page. Titles include, *How to Run Your Own Restaurant, Running Your Own Boarding Kennels, Running Your Own Catering Company, Running Your Own Hairdressing Salon, Running Your Own Mail Order Business, Running Your Own Market Stall, Running Your Own Photographic Business, Running Your Own Playgroup or Nursery, Running Your Own Pub, Running Your Own Shop, Running Your Own Small Hotel.*

Signposts, Careers and Occupational Information Centre, Sheffield. A comprehensive card index of occupations based on *CODOT*.

Working Abroad, Godfrey Golzen, London, Kogan Page.

CAREER PLANNING/LIFE PLANNING BOOKS

Build Your Own Rainbow B. Hopson, and M. Scally, London, Lifeskills Associates.

Career Change, L. Morphy, CRAC, Cambridge, Hobsons Press. This guide includes self-assessment flow charts as well as information on professional-level careers.

Career Tracking, Jimmy Calano and Jeff Salzman, Aldershot, Gower.

Changing Your Job After 35, G. Golzen, London, Kogan Page.

How to Choose a Career, Vivien Donald, London, Kogan Page.

Manage your Own Career, B. Ball, London, Kogan Page. Information on the current employment scene and questionnaires on your interests, etc.

Portable Careers, Linda R. Greenbury, London, Kogan Page.

Putting Redunancy Behind You – A Life and Career Strategy, S. Cane and P. Lowman, London, Kogan Page.

Self-Empowerment, How to Get What You Want From Life, Sam R. Lloyd and Christine Berthelot, London Kogan Page.

Springboard: Women's Development Workbook, L. Willis, J. Daisley, Stroud, Hawthorn Press. A morale-builder and source of ideas and information.

Taking Stock: Being Fifty in the Eighties, C. Handy, London, BBC Publications.

The Best is Yet to Come, M. Smith, London, Lifeskills Associates. A workbook for the middle years.

The Manager's Self-Assessment Kit, Ernst & Young, London, Kogan Page.

The Mid-Career Action Guide, Derek and Fred Kemp, London, Kogan Page.

What Colour's Your Parachute? R. Bolles (annual) London, 10 Speed Press, (UK version from Umbrella Publications). An entertaining 'manual' for job-hunters and career changers.

CHILDREN/YOUTH

Advice, Advocacy and Representation Service for Children. 1 Sickle Street, Manchester M60 2AA. Tel: 061-839 8442. ASC is there for any child/young person who needs confidential advice.

Advisory Centre for Education (ACE). 1B Aberdeen Studios, 22–24 Highbury Grove, London N5 2EA. Helpline: 071 354 8321. An independent national advice centre that provides free advice, information and support to parents in maintained schools.

Anti-Bullying Campaign. 10 Borough High Street, London SE1 9QQ. Helpline: 071-378 1446. Helps parents with step-by-step guidelines on how to work with schools to combat the problems of bullying.

Barnado's. Tanners Lane, Barkingside, Ilford, Essex IG6 1QS. Tel: 081-550 68822. The services offered include fostering, adoption, emergency accommodation for homeless young people and respite care, education and training for disabled children and young people.

Brook Advisory Centres. 153A East Street, London SE17 2SD. Tel: 071-708 1234. Twenty-six local centres provide a confidential counselling and contraceptive service for young people.

Centrepoint. 2 Swallow Place, Bewlay House, Oxford Circus, London W1R 7AA. Tel: 071-629 2229. Provides good quality housing and support for homeless young people.

Childline. 2nd Floor, Royal Mail Building, Studd Street, London N1 0QW. Tel: 071-239 1000 (Helpline: 0800 1111). Childline is the UK's only free national helpline for children in trouble or danger. The charity, provides a 24 hour confidential counselling service.

The Children's Legal Centre Ltd. 20 Compton Terrace, London N1 2UN. Helpline: 071-359 6521. An independent national organisation, concerned with law and policy affecting young people in England and Wales.

The Children's Society. Edward Rudolf House, Margery Street, London WC1X 0JL. Tel: 071-837 4299. A national voluntary child care organisation which works with and for children, young people and families to tackle disadvantage and to promote child welfare and development.

Childwatch. 206 Hessle Road, Hull, North Humberside HU3 3BE. Helpline 0482 25552. An education and prevention unit which refers cases of abuse to the police and social services. It also counsels adults who have been abused as children.

Cry-Sis. BM CRY-SIS, London WC1N 3XX. Tel: 071-404 5011. Offers self-help and support for families with excessively crying, sleepless and demanding children. Publications are available, enclose SAE when writing.

Enureses and Resource Information Centre. 65 St. Michaels Hill, Bristol BS2 8DZ. Helpline: 0272 264920. ERIC is a national charity providing advice for children and teenagers, parents and professionals on bed wetting and day-time wetting.

Kidscape. 152 Buckingham Palace Rd, London SW1W 9TR. Helpline: 071-730 3300. Deals with bullying, getting lost, stranger danger and threats of abuse from known adults.

Kids Clubs Network. 279-281 Whitechapel Road, London E1 1BY. Tel: 071-247 3009. Can put parents and employers in touch with their local clubs and through publications and training, can assist those wanting to establish new clubs.

National Council for Voluntary Youth Services. Coborn House, 3 Coborn Road, London E3 2DA. Tel: 081-980 5712. NCVYS can help find an appropriate youth organisation anywhere in England.

National Council of YMCAs. 640 Forest Road, London E17 3DZ. Tel: 081-520 5599. One of the country's largest youth welfare charities. It provides housing for the homeless, training for the unemployed, counselling for the abused and sports facilities for all.

NCH Action for Children. 85 Highbury Park, London N5 1UD. Tel: 071-226 2033. NCH Action for Children runs over 200 projects throughout the UK, which include family centres, abuse, disability and homelessness projects.

NCH Action for Children – Scotland. 17 Newton Place, Glasgow G3 7PY. Tel: 041 332 4041. Runs over 30 projects throughout Scotland which include family centres, child protection, disability, homelessness, mediation and criminal justice projects.

Network '81. 1-7 Woodfield Terrace, Chapel Hill, Stanstead, Essex CM24 8AJ. Helpline: 0279 647415. A national network of parents of children with special educational needs, offering help and advice within support groups for parents and raising public awareness of the need for integration.

NSPCC. 67 Saffron Hill, London EC1N 8RS. Helpline 0800 800500. Through it's national helpline, teams and projects, the NSPCC works to protect and support abused children and their families.

Pre-School Playgroups Association. 61-63 Kings Cross Road, London WC1X 9LL. Tel: 071-833 0991. (Helpline 071-837 0991). The Association's member groups provide the opportunity for under fives to learn through play and offer support for playgroups through training, fieldworkers and literature. The helpline is for parents seeking childcare facilities.

Parents Against Injustice (PAIN). 3 Riverside Business Park, Stanstead, Essex CM24 8PL. Tel: 0279 647171. PAIN supports and advises parents, family and children when a child is mistakenly thought to be at risk or to have been abused. They liaise with solicitors/child-care practitioners and doctors prepared to give a second medical or psychiatric opinions.

Royal Scottish Society for Prevention of Cruelty to Children (RSSPCC). 41 Polwarth Terrace, Edinburgh EH11 1NU. Tel: 031-337 8539. An independent, voluntary organisation whose aim is to prevent the abuse and neglect of children and to protect the interest and welfare of those who may be at risk in Scotland.

'Who Cares?' Scotland. Block 5 Unit C3, Templeton Business Centre, Templeton Street Glasgow G40 1DA. Tel: 041-554 4452. Run by and for young people with experience in care. Their aim is to make life better for young people in care by helping them to express their views and wishes to the appropriate authority.

'Who Cares?' Trust. Citybridge House, 235-245 Goswell Road, London EC1V 7DJ. Tel: 071-833 9047. Provides advice and information for young people and those who work with them.

Youth Access. Magazine Business Centre, 11 Newarke Street, Leicester LE1 5SS. Tel: 0533 558763. Provides a national referral service for all young people to their local advice and counselling service.

Young Women's Christian Associations of Great Britain (YWCA of GB). Clarendon House, 52 Cornmarket Street, Oxford OX1 3EJ. Tel: 0865 726110. An informed membership movement working at local, national and international levels to enable women and young people to take greater control over their lives.

COPING

(See also the 'ADVICE' section of the appendix)

Relate (National Marriage Guidance). See your telephone directory or contact: Relate, Herbert Gray College, Little Church Street, Rugby CV21 3AP. Tel: 0788 573241 or 0788 560811. Counselling and Advice for Couples (married or not, heterosexual or gay).

The Samaritans. See your telephone directory.

Your GP.

DISABILITIES

AFASIC. 347 Central Markets, Smithfield, London EC1A 9NH. Tel: 071-236 3632. Represents children and young people with speech and language impairments. It aims to improve educational provision, training and employment opportunities.

Association to Aid Sexual and Personal Relationships of People with a Disability (SPOD) 286 Camden Road, London N7 0BJ. Helpline: 071-607 8851. SPOD offers counselling to disabled people who are experiencing problems in their personal and/or sexual relationships. It also offers training and support for professional carers.

Association for Spina Bifida and Hydrocephalus. 42 Park Road, Peterborough PE1 2UQ. Tel: 0733 555988. Provides practical help and information to individuals with Spina Bifida and/or Hydrocephalus and their families. Trained fieldworkers visit families and specialist advisers help with mobility, continence, education, etc.

Scottish Spina Bifida Association. 190 Queensferry Road, Edinburgh EH4 2BW. Tel: 031 332 0743. They seek to increase public awareness and understanding of individuals with Spina Bifida/Hydrocephalus and allied disorders.

Benefits Agency. Quarry House, Quarry Hill, Leeds LS2 7UA. DSS Disability Benefits line: 0800 882200. They are responsible for paying Social Security benefits and providing free telephone advice on the number above.

Contact-a-Family. 16 Strutton Ground, London SW1P 2HP. Helpline 071-222 2695. A national charity providing information and support for parents of children with disabilities. It has a network of support groups offering information about rare conditions and syndromes, with useful publications and a helpline.

DIALUK (Disablement Information and Advice Line). Park Lodge, St Catherine's Hospital, Tickhill Road, Balby, Doncaster, S Yorks DN4 8QN. Tel: 0302 310123. The HQ of a network of 100 disability centres, giving free, independent advice on all aspects of disability.

Disability Scotland. Princes House, 5 Shandwick Place, Edinburgh EH2 4RG. Tel: 031 229 8632. The national voluntary organisation representing people with a disability in Scotland.

Disabled Living Foundation. 380–384 Harrow Road, London W9 2HU. Tel: 071-289 6111. A national charity providing practical, up-to-date advice and information on all aspects of living with disability for disabled and elderly people and their carers.

Down's Syndrome Association. 153–155 Mitcham Road, London SW17 9PG. Office and Helpline: 081-682 4001. A registered charity with branches and groups throughout England, Wales and Northern Ireland.

Scottish Down's Syndrome Association. 158–160 Balgreen Road, Edinburgh, EH11 3AU. Tel: 031-313 4225. Aims to provide support for people with Down's Syndrome and their families, and to increase public awareness and understanding.

The Foundation for Conductive Education. Calthorpe House, 30 Hagley Road, Edgbaston, Birmingham B16 8QY. Tel: 021-456 5533. In partnership with the Peto Institute, Hungary, the Foundation is a national charity which provides Conductive Education for children with Cerebral Palsy and adults with other motor disorders.

Holiday Care Service. 2 Old Bank Chambers, Station Road, Horley, Surrey RG6 9HW. Helpline: 0293 774535. The UK's central resource on information about holidays for disabled and older people, one parent families and those disadvantaged by low income.

MENCAP. Mencap National Centre, 123 Golden Lane, London EC1Y ORT. Tel: 071 454 0454. The UK's largest organisation for people with a learning disability and their families/carers, providing high quality services, advice and support.

Mobility Information Service. National Mobility Centre, Unit 2a Atcham Estate, Shresbury SY4 4UG. Tel: 0743 761889. Provides advice to the disabled, offering driver assessments, a range of adapted vehicles and information packs for drivers and passengers.

The National Autistic Society. 276 Willesden Lane, London NW2 5RB. Tel: 081-451 1114. Owns and manages schools and centres for people with autism and offers a diagnostic and assessment service, gives advice and information, produces literature and supports a research information unit.

PHAB (Physically Disabled and Able Bodied). 12-14 London Road, Croydon, Surrey CR0 2TO. Tel: 081-567 5510. PHAB covers the whole of the UK and works mainly through PHAB clubs in local communities. They allow people with and without disabilities to meet together to achieve total integration.

RADAR (The Royal Association for Disability and Rehabilitation). 12 City Forum, 250 City Road, London EC1V 8AF. Tel: 071-250 3222. RADAR seeks to remove the architectural, economic and attitudinal barriers faced by disabled people, specialising in the areas of mobility, education, employment, social services, housing and social security.

Royal National Institute for Deaf People. 105 Gower Street, London WC1E 6AH. Tel: 071-387 8033. Provides a range of services for deaf and hard of hearing people and their families, interpreting services, Typetalk, residential care, assertive devices and comprehensive information.

Royal National Institute for the Blind (RNIB). 224 Great Portland Street, London W1N 6AA. Tel: 071-388 1266. RNIB's task is to challenge blindness. They challenge the disabling effects of sight loss by providing information and over 60 services to help people to get on with their own lives.

DRESS AND BODY LANGUAGE

Colour Me Beautiful, 66 Abbey Business Centre, Ingate Place, London SW8 3NS Tel 071- 627 5211: Seminars Books and Careers as Image Consultants.

Discover Your Colours, video presented by Mary Spillane and distributed by Chrysalis Video.

The Complete Style Guide, London, by Judy Piatkus (Publishers) Ltd.

The Image Factor – A Guide to Effective Self-Presentation, Eleri Sampson, London, Kogan Page.

DRUGS AND ADDICTIONS

ADFAM National. Chapel House, 18 Hatton Place, London EC1N 8ND. Helpline: 071-405 3923. Runs a national telephone helpline for the families and friends of drug users, offering confidential support and information.

Al-Anon Family Groups UK & Eire. 61 Great Dover Street, London SE1 4YS. Helpline: 071-403 0888. Helps provide support for relatives and friends of alcoholics. Alateen, as part of Al-Anon, is for teenagers who are affected by the drinking problem of a relative/close friend.

Alcoholics Anonymous. Stonebow House, Stonebow, York Y01 2NJ. Tel: 0904 644026. AA is a fellowship of men and women who share their experiences with each other so that they may solve their common problems and help others to recover from alcoholism.

CITA (Council for Involuntary Tranquilliser Addiction). Cavendish House, Brighton Road, Waterloo, Liverpool L22 5NG. Helpline: 051-949 0102. Offers support and information to the sufferers from addiction of prescribed drugs, primarily tranquillisers, and to families of these sufferers.

Drinkline (The National Alcohol Helpline). 13–14 West Smithfield, London EC1A 9DH. Tel: 071 332 0150. Provides information and advice to callers worried about their own drinking, support to the family and friends of people who are drinking and advice on where to go for help.

Families Anonymous. Unit 37, Doddington & Rollo Community Association, Charlotte Despard Avenue, London SW11 5JE. Tel: 071-498 4680. Families Anonymous self-help groups are for those affected by drug or the related problems of a relative or friend.

Gamblers Anonymous and Gam-Anon. PO Box 88, London SW10 0EU. Helpline: 071-384 3040. A self-help fellowship of men and women who have joined together to do something about their gambling problems. Gam-Anon offers friendship, practical help, comfort and understanding to families of compulsive gamblers.

Narcotics Anonymous. PO Box 1980, London N19 3LS. Tel: 071-272 9040. Offers help to any individual who wants to stop using drugs. Their message is that any addict can stop using drugs, lose the desire to use, and find a new way to live.

QUIT. 102 Gloucester Place, London W1H 3DA. Tel: 071-487 3000. Quitline, run by the charity QUIT, offers non-judgemental help and advice to smokers wishing to quit and ex-smokers who are looking for additional and ongoing support.

Release. 388 Old Street, London EC1V 9LT. Helpline: 071-729 9904. The national drugs and legal advice service. Provides a 24 hour telephone Helpline for drug users and their families and friends, giving confidential advice and information.

Re-Solv. 30A High Street, Stone, Staffordshire ST15 8AW. Tel: 0785 817885. They contribute to a healthier, happier and safer social environment by preventing death, suffering and crime, which may result as a consequence of solvent and volatile substance abuse.

The Standing Conference on Drug Abuse (SCODA). 1-4 Hatton Place, Hatton Garden, London EC1 8ND. Tel: 071-430 2341. SCODA is able to give up-to-date information on local specialist services. Information is free and available to drug users, their families, friends and also to interested professionals.

Turning Point. 101 Back Church Lane, London E1 1LU. Tel: 071-702 2300. The largest national charity helping people with drink, drug and mental health problems. It operates over 45 services, offering residential rehabilitation, day care and street level advice.

DIRECTORIES – POTENTIAL EMPLOYERS (UK and Overseas)

Check the reference section of your local library.
The City Directory, Director Books, Hemel Hempstead.
Crawford's Directory of City Connections, Crawford Publications Ltd, London.
Current British Directories, CBD Research, Beckenham, Kent.
Directory of British Associations, CBD Research, Beckenham, Kent.
Directory of Training Support Services, Kogan Page, London.
Extel Card Service, Extel Statistical Services, London.
Financial Times International Business Yearbook, *Financial Times*, London.
Kompass Register of British Industries and Commerce, CRI, London.

ELDERLY

Abbeyfield Society. 186–192 Darkes Lane, Potters Bar, Herts EN6 1AB. Tel: 0707 644845. Provides independent living and care for older people no longer willing or able to live alone. Residents are supported by a resident housekeeper who provides the main meals.

Age Concern – England, Wales, Scotland and Northern Ireland. Astral House, 1268 London Road, London SW16 4ER. Tel: 081-679 8000. Provides direct services to older people in the UK, including day care, advice, fact-sheets and books.

Anchor Housing Association. Anchor House, 269A Banbury Road, Oxford OX2 7HU. Tel: 0865 311511. Provides sheltered housing, residential care, advice and practical help to older home owners to improve and adapt their properties.

Care & Repair Limited. Castle House, Kirtley Drive, Nottingham NG7 1LD. Tel: 0602 799091. Co-ordinates around 150 Home Improvement Agencies countrywide. They help people who are elderly, disabled and/or living on low income to repair or adapt their homes.

Counsel and Care. Twyman House, 16 Bonny Street, London NW1 9PG. Tel: 071-485 1566. Provides a free advice service for older people and their families, including welfare benefits, accommodation and help at home.

Help the Aged. St James's Walk, London EC1R 0BE. Tel: 0800 289404. Help the Aged works to improve the quality of life of elderly people in the UK and internationally, particularly those who are frail, isolated or poor.

EX-ARMED FORCES

If you have served in the armed forces for a period of three years or more at **any** time in your life the following will be able to help:

The Regular Forces Employment Association. Head Office: 25 Bloomsbury Square, London WC1A 2LN. Tel 071-637 3918. Telephone or write for your local branch. There are 40 throughout the UK.

SSAFA. Head Office: 19 Queen Elizabeth Street, London SE1 2LP. Tel: 071-403 8783. Telephone or write for your local branch – there are hundreds throughout the UK. Offers help from a friendly chat to liaising with the gas company about payment arrears, etc.

FAMILY

Asian Family Counselling. 74 The Avenue, London W13 8LB. Tel: 081-997 5749. A charity which assists Asian families with marital problems and offers professional counselling, and also assists in arranging contact between children and divorced parents.

British Agencies for Adoption and Fostering (BAAF). 11 Southwark Street, London SE1 1RQ. Tel: 071-407 8800. BAAF aims to ensure public and professional understanding of the issues in adoption and fostering.

British Dyslexia Association. 98 London Road, Reading, Berkshire RG1 5AU. Helpline: 0734 668271. The BDA provides support and information to all those with dyslexia – children, adults, their parents, families and professionals in education and employment.

The Compassionate Friends. 53 North Street, Bristol BS3 1EN. Tel: 0272 665202. An organisation of parents whose child of any age, including adults, has died through accident, illness, murder or suicide. They offer friendship and understanding from other bereaved parents through personal or group support.

Cruse (Bereavement Care). Cruse House, 126 Sheen Road, Richmond, Surrey TW9 1UR. Tel: 081-940 4818. Offers free help to all bereaved people by providing both individual and group counselling, opportunities for social contact and practical advice.

Exploring Parenthood (EP). Latimer Education Centre, 194 Freston Road, London W10 6TT. Tel: 081-960 1678. Provides professional support and advice to all parents, with easy access to professional advice and support, preventing problems from developing into crisis.

Families Need Fathers. 134 Curtain Road, London EC2A 3AR. Tel: 071-613-5060. A registered charity which offers advice, support and representation to parents (particularly non-custodials) in maintaining a sound parent/child relationship in divorce/separation.

Family Rights Group (England and Wales). The Print House, 18 Ashwin Street, London E8 3DL. Advice/Helpline: 071-249 0008. Promotes partnerships between families and child care agencies in England and Wales, offering confidential advice and information.

Family Service Unit. 207 Marylebone Road, London NW1 5QP. Tel: 071-402 5175. Services include playschemes, furniture and clothing, advice on housing, welfare benefits and immigration, and counselling on family breakdown, sexual or other forms of abuse.

Family Welfare Association. 501-505 Kingsland Road, London E8 4AU. Tel: 071-254 6251. Assists families to overcome the effects of poverty, providing practical, emotional and financial support. It also promotes professional social work practice and training.

FFLAG – Families and Friends and Gays. PO Box 153, Manchester M60 1LP. Helplines: 061-628 7621, 0533 708331. Provides confidential support for parents and their gay, lesbian and bi-sexual sons or daughters.

Home Start UK. 2 Salisbury Road, Leicester LE7 7QR. Tel: 0533 554988. Volunteers offer regular support, friendship and practical help to young families under stress in their own homes, helping to prevent family crisis and breakdown.

Gingerbread. 35 Wellington Street, London WC2E 7BN. Advice Line: 071-240 0953. The national organisation for lone parents and their children. It has over 500 support groups throughout the UK.

Missing Persons Bureau. Roebuck House, 284-286 Upper Richmond Road West, East Sheen, London SW14 7JE. Tel: 081-392 2000. Aims to provide practical help and support for families of missing persons, helping them to regain contact, offering publicity advice and information.

National Council for One Parent Families. 255 Kentish Town Road, London NW5 2LX. Tel: 071-267 1361. Experts on all issues of one-parent family life and social employment policy issues affecting lone parents.

National Stepfamily Association (Stepfamily). 72 Willesden Lane, London NW6 7TA. Tel: 071-372 0844. Offers advice, support and information to all members of stepfamilies and those who work with them, supporting step-parenting, encouraging research on remarriage.

Norcap (National Organisation for Counselling Adoptees and their parents). 3 New High Street, Headington, Oxford OX3 7AJ. Helpline: 0865 750554. Provides support, guidance and sympathetic understanding to adult adoptees and their birth and adoptive parents.

Parentline. Westbury, 57 Hart Road, Thundersley, Essex SS7 3PP. Helpline: 0268 757077. Provides support for parents under stress, therefore maximising a family's capacity to care for its children.

Parent Network. 44–46 Caversham Road, London NW5 2DS. Tel: 071-485 8535. The Parent-Link programme equips parents to feel supported and encouraged, by offering ways to make changes which can improve relationships within the family.

Refuge. Tel: 081-747 0133. Crisis line: 081-994 9952. Offers emergency accommodation, nursery and after-school facilities, one-to-one counselling, and a seven day a week playcentre during the summer holidays.

Relate-National Marriage Guidance. Herbert Gray College, Little Church Street, Rugby, Warwickshire CV21 3AP. Tel: 0788 573241. Relate, the leading marital counselling agency in the UK, helps over 70,000 couples in distress every year.

Survivors of Sexual Abuse. Feltham Open Door Project, The Debrome Building, Boundaries Road, Feltham TW13 5DT. Helpline: 081-890 4732. Provides services to male and female survivors of sexual abuse, offering face-to-face counselling. Regular self-help groups are available and a 24 hour helpline answerphone.

FINANCIAL ADVISERS

The following organisations will supply you with a list of registered independent Financial Advisers in your area.

FIMBRA. (The Financial Intermediaries Managers and Brokers Regulatory Association). Hertsmere House, Hertsmere Road, London E14 4AB. Tel: 071-538 8860.

IFA Ltd. 4th Floor, Greville Street, London EC1N 8SU. Tel: 0483 461461. Leave name, address and postcode to receive a listing of six local Independent Financial Advisers.

HEALTH

Alzheimer's Disease Society. Gordon House, 10 Greencoat Place, London SW1P 1PH. Tel: 071-306 0606. Provides advice and information to carers and families, and campaigns for better services, supports research and undertakes fundraising.

Alzheimer's Scotland. 8 Hill Street, Edinburgh EH2 3JZ. Tel: 031-225 1453. Provides advice and information to carers and families. It campaigns for better services, supports research and undertakes fundraising.

Association for Post Natal Illness. 25 Jerdan Place, Fulham, London SW61 1BE. Helpline: 071-386 0868. Offers telephone support on a one-to-one basis for women suffering with Post Natal Depression, from women who have recovered from PND. Information packs are available free of charge (with an SAE).

British Association of Cancer United Patients (BACUP). 3 Bath Place, Rivington Street, London EC2A 3JR. Tel: 071-696 9003. Provides a free and confidential service including a telephone helpline, counselling service, and booklets on cancer.

British Diabetic Association. 10 Queen Anne Street, London W1M 0BD. Helpline: 071-323 1531. Helps people with diabetes and supports diabetes research.

British Epilepsy Organisation. Anstey House, 40 Hannover Square, Leeds LS3 1BE. Tel: 0352 089599. The national charity providing care in the community for the country's estimated 300,000 people with epilepsy.

British Migraine Association. 178A High Road, Byfleet, West Byfleet, Surrey KT14 7ED. Helpline: 0932 352468. Supports research and provides encouragement and information which enables many migraine sufferers to control their attacks and live normal lives.

Cancerlink. 17 Britannia Street, London WC1X 9JN. Tel: 071-833 2451. In Scotland: 9 Castle Terrace, Edinburgh EH1 2DP. Tel: 031-228 5557. Aims to offer emotional support and information to people affected by cancer, their relatives and professionals working with them.

Chest, Heart and Stroke Scotland. Tel: 031-225 6963. Funds research projects and supports health education programmes, rehabilitation projects, and gives advice and support to those who suffer from these illnesses.

Council for Complimentary & Alternative Medicine. 179 Gloucester Place, London NW1 6DX. Tel: 071-724 9103. Aim is to ensure safety of the public by ensuring those who practise non-orthodox medicine are fully qualified practitioners, bound by strict codes of ethics and practice and are fully insured. For information send an SAE and cheque for £1.50.

Cystic Fibrosis Trust. Alexandra House, 5 Blyth Road, Bromley, Kent BR1 3RS. Tel: 081-4647 211. Funds vital research into improved treatment and prevention of CF, and provides a comprehensive support network producing extensive literature.

Department of Health. Richmond House, 79 Whitehall, London SW1A 2NS. For health information: 0800 665544. For health literature: 0800 555777. The health information service line is for any health-related enquiry. The healthline is for health-related literature.

Eating Disorders Association. Sackville Place, 44 Magdalen Street, Norwich, Norfolk NR3 1JU. Helpline: 0603 621414. Offers information and understanding to everyone who is involved with bulimia or anorexia through helplines, self-help groups, or individual membership .

ENABLE (Formerly Scottish Society for the Mentally Handicapped). Tel: 041-226 4541. Offers support, legal advice, information, respite care, holidays, homes, jobs and self-advocacy training for people with learning disabilities and their families.

Epilepsy Association of Scotland. 48 Govan Road, Glasgow G51 1JL. Tel: 041-427 4911. A charity committed to improving the life quality of people with epilepsy in Scotland.

Family Heart Association. 7 High Street, Kidlington, Oxon OX5 2DH. Tel: 0865 370292. A national charity helping families who inherit a high blood cholesterol and others at high risk of coronary heart disease.

Food and Chemical Allergy Association. 27 Ferringham Lane, Ferring-by-Sea West Sussex BN12 5NB. A booklet, 'Understanding Allergies', is available on receipt of £2.00 plus a medium-sized SAE. Other information and advice is available on writing to Mrs Ellen Rothera at the above address.

Foundation for the Study of Infant Cot Death. Head Office: 35 Belgrave Square, London SW1X 8QB. Helpline: 071-235 1721. Raises funds for research into cot death, support bereaved families and puts parents in touch with local befrienders.

Headway. 7 King Edward Court, King Edward Street, Nottingham NG1 1EW. Helpline: 0602 240800. Provides day-care services, advice and information to people with head injuries. Headway also campaigns to reduce the incidence of head injury.

Hodgkin's Disease Association. PO Box 275, Haddenham, Aylesbury, Bucks HP17 8JJ. Helpline: 0844 291500. Provides information and emotional support for Hodgkin's Disease and Non-Hodgkin's Lymphoma patients and their families.

ME Association. Stanhope House, High Street, Stanford-Le-Hope, Essex SS17 0HA. Advice Line: 0375 361013. Provides advice and support to people affected by ME, promotes research into cause and effect, and increases public awareness.

MIND. Grants House, 15–19 Broadway, Stratford London E15 4BQ. Tel: 081-519 2122. Provides services ranging from counselling to housing projects, for people with mental health problems and their families and friends.

Multiple Slerocis Society of Great Britain and Northern Ireland. 25 Effie Road, Fulham, London SW6 1EE. Tel: 071-736 6267. Helpline: 071-371 8000. With a network of 370 branches, the MS Society funds research to find the cause and cure of MS.

National Aids Helpline. PO Box 1577, London NW1 3DW. Helpline: 0800 567123. All calls are free and confidential and you can call at any time to talk with a trained adviser.

National Asthma Campaign. Providence House, Providence Place, London N1 0NT. Tel: 071-226 2260. Helpline: 0345 010203. Provides information and support on all aspects of asthma, to people with asthma, their friends, family and health professionals.

National Eczema Society. 4 Tavistock Place, London WC1H 9RA. Tel: 071-388 4097. Promotes and advocates quality care through the provision of information, support and education. Also funds research to find the causes and cures for eczema.

National Kidney Federation. 6 Stanley Street, Workshop, Notts S81 7HX. Tel: 0909 487795. Provides advice and information to kidney patients on matters relating to renal failure, dialysis and transplantation.

National Meningitis Trust. Fern House, Bath Road, Stroud, Glos GL5 3TJ. Helpline: 0453 755049. Aims to raise money for research, provides help and support and increases awareness among the public and health professionals.

Parkinson's Disease Society of the UK. 22 Upper Woburn Place, London WC1H 0RA. Tel: 071-383 3513. Helpline: 071-388 5798. Aims to conquer the disease, alleviate the suffering and distress it causes through research, education, welfare and communication.

Phobic Action. Claybury Grounds, Manor Road, Woodford Green, Essex 1GB 8PR. Helpline: 081-559 2459. Offers practical help and support to people with anxiety disorders and their carers, using self-help, self-treatment methods and home visits where possible.

Positively Women. 5 Sebastian Street, London EC1V 0HE. Tel: 071-490 5515. Helpline: 071-490 2327. Provides a range of free and strictly confidential support to women with HIV or AIDS, offering information and advice on Welfare Rights and alternative therapies.

Saneline. 199–205 Old Marleybone Road, London NW1 5QP. Helpline: 071-724 8000. Provides confidential support, information and help to anyone coping with mental illness.

Scottish Association for Mental Health (SAMH). Atlantic House, 38 Gardners Crescent, Edinburgh EH3 8DQ. Tel: 031-229 9687. Campaigns for better hospital and community services, seeking to increase understanding of mental distress and promote mental health.

The Spastics Society. 12 Park Crescent, London W1N 4EQ. Tel: 071-636 5020. Helpline: 0800 626216. Is a large charity providing care, accommodation, therapy, and education.

Scottish Council for Spastics. ETAS Centre, 11 Ellersly Road, Edinburgh EH12 6HY. Tel: 031-313 5510. Exists to enable the needs of people with cerebral palsy and those with a disability resulting in similar needs to be met.

The Stroke Association. CHSA House, Whitecross Street, London EC1Y 8JJ. Helpline: 071-490 7999. Helps stroke patients and their families through advice, publications, welfare grants, local groups and in some areas visiting services.

Terrance Higgins Trust. 52–54 Gray's Inn Road, London WC1X 8JU. Tel: 071-831 0330. Helpline: 071-242 1010. Provides legal, welfare rights advice, counselling and buddying services to people infected or affected with HIV or AIDS, and also health promotion materials.

Young Minds. 22A Boston Place, London NW1 6ER. Helpline: 0345 626376. Works to promote the mental health of children, young people and their families, acting as an umbrella body for mental health professionals and provides information to the public.

JOBSEARCH BOOKS

Answer The Question: Get the Job!, Iain Maitland, London, Random House.

Britains Best Employers?, Sean Hamil, London, Kogan Page.

'Careers In ...', series of books for school-leavers, (e.g. *Careers in Radio & TV*), London, Kogan Page.

Changing Your Job After 35, Godfrey Golzen and Philip Plumbley, London, Kogan Page.

Company Magazine's Top 100 Jobs, Suzanne Askham, London, Random House.

Coping with Interviews, by Martin Higham, The New Opportunity Press (76 St James' Lane, London N10 3RD).

First Find Your Hilltop, take control of your career by finding out who you are, where you want to be and how to get there, London, Hutchinson.

Get That Job! by Iran Hussell and John Kellett, Edinburgh, MacDonald (Edgefield Road, Loanhead, Midlothian EH20 9SY).

Getting There, Jobhunting for Women, Margaret Wallis, London, Kogan Page.

Great Answers to Tough Interview Questions, Yate, London, Kogan Page.

How to be a Good Judge of Character, D. M. Davey, London, Kogan Page.

How to be Headhunted, Yvonne Sarch, London, Random House.

How to Get A Job, by Marjorie Harris, London, the Institute of Personnel Management (IPM House, Camp Road, Wimbledon, London SW19 4UW).

How to Get a Job after 45, Daily Telegraph, London, Kogan Page .

How to Master Selection Tests, Mike Bryon and Sanjay Modha, London, Kogan Page.

How to Suceed in a Highly Competitive Job Market, Brian Croucher, London, Kogan Page.

How to Win at Jobhunting, Iain Maitland, London, Random House.

How to Win at Interviews, Iain Maitland, London, Random House.

How to Write a Winning CV, Alan Jones, London, Random House.

How You Can Get That Job!, Rebecca Corfield, London, Kogan Page. *Improving Your Presentation Skills*, M. Stevens, London, Kogan Page.

Interviews, Skills and strategy, J. Courtis, London, IPM Books.

Job Hunting Made Easy, J. Bramham and D. Cox, London, Kogan Page.

JobKey, (annual), The New Opportunity Press (76 St James' Lane, London N10 3RD).

Jobs in a Jobless World, Godfrey Golzen. Published by Frederick Muller (Dataday House, 8 Alexandria Road, Wimbledon, London SW19 7JZ).

Perfect CV, Max Eggert, London, Random House.

Perfect Interview, Max Eggert, Random House.

Preparing Your Own CV, Rebecca Corfield, London, Kogan Page.

Sucessful Interviews, Rebecca Corfield, London, Kogan Page.

Tactics for Changing Your Life, A. Kidman, London, Kogan Page.

Technical Selection Tests and How to Pass Them, M. Byron and S. Modha, London, Kogan Page.

Test Your Executive Skills, T. Farnsworth, London, Ebury Press. Assess your potential with 50 quizzes.

Test Your Management IQ, Colby, London, Pan.

The Expatriate's Handbook, B. Twinn and P. Burns, London, Kogan Page.

The Job Assault Course, M.S. Lindsay Stewart, London, Kogan Page.

The Manager's Book of Checklists, a practical guide to improve your managerial skills, D. Rowntree, London, Gower.

Your Job Search, P. Gaudet, M. Estier and E. Riera, London, Kogan Page.

Your Next Move, Philip Pedley and Paul McEvoy, London, Kogan Page.

LIBRARIES

Westminster Central Reference Library, St Martin's Street, London WC2H 7HP. Tel: 071-798 2034.

City Business Library, 106 Fenchurch Street, London EC2. Tel: 071-638 8215. Publishes two useful free guides to reference material: 'Company Information in the City Business Library' which covers both British and overseas companies and 'Market Research Sources in the City Business Library'.

Science Reference and Information Service, Business Information Service Section, 25 Southampton Buildings, Chancery Lane, London WC2A 1AN. Tel. 071-323 7454.

Manchester Central Library, St Peter's Square, Manchester M2 5PD. Tel: 061-236 9422.

Birmingham Central Library, Chamberlain Square, Birmingham B3 3HQ. Tel: 021-235 4511.

Edinburgh Central Library, George IV Bridge, Edinburgh EH1 1EG. Tel: 031-225 5584.

Glasgow District Libraries HQ, The Mitchell Library, North Street, Glasgow G3 7DN. Tel. 041-221 7030.

Other libraries

Export Market Information Centre, British Overseas Trade Board, 1 Victoria Street, London SW1H 0ET. Tel: 071-215 5444. Has useful information on exports.

The Library at the King's Fund Centre, 126 Albert Street, London NW1 7NF. Tel: 071-267 6111. Has a large collection of material on health, social service and voluntary organisations.

Local Government Information Service (LOGIS), which can be contacted at County Halls, provides information to those in local government on political, local government services, legislation and management.

If you are a member of a professional institute, e.g., The Institute of Management, you will have access to their library (and also possibly their career counselling service).

If your old college/university is close why not make use of the library there? If not, try the local university or college – turn up in person, it's a lot easier for them to refuse you over the telephone!

And, of course, your local library.

ORGANISATIONS

Alliance of Small Firms and Self-employed People: 33 The Green, Calne, Wilts SN11 8DJ.

Association of British Chambers of Commerce. Sovereign House, 212a Shaftesbury Avenue, London WC2H 8EW.

Association of Independent Businesses, Trowbray House, 108 Weston Street, London SE1 3QB.

British Franchise Association. Franchise Chambers, Thames View, Newtown Road, Henley-on-Thames, Oxon RG9 1HG.

Institute of Directors. 116 Pall Mall, London SW1Y 5ED.

Institute of Small Businesses. 14 Willow St, London EC2A 4BH.

Investors in Industry plc. 91 Waterloo Road, London SE1 8XP.

London Enterprise Agency. 4 Snow Hill, London EC1A 2BS.

National Federation of Self-employed and Small Businesses. 32 St Anne's Road West, Lytham St Anne's, Lancs FY8 1NY

PERSONALITY AND OTHER EVALUATIONS

Personality types

Please Understand Me, David Keirsey and Marilyn Bates, Delmar, California, Prometheus Nemesis Books.

Life Types, Sandra Hirsh and Jean Kummerow, New York, NY, Warner.

If you have difficulty obtaining either of the above contact: Oxford Psychologists Press, Tel: 0865 510203.

Team types

Management Teams: Why They Succeed or Fail, Dr Meredith Belbin, Oxford, Butterworth-Heinemann. Available directly from: Belbin Associates, 52 Burleigh Street, Cambridge, CB1 1DJ. Tel: 0223 60895.

RECRUITMENT GUIDES

CEPEC Recruitment Guide, A directory of Recruitment Agencies and Search Consultants in the United Kingdom. Available directly from CEPEC, Tel: 071-930 0322 (approx. £20).

REDUNDANCY

Your Employment Rights, Michael Malone, London, Kogan Page.

Employers are given the following advice by **ACAS – The Advisory, Conciliation and Arbitration Service**.

When faced with redundancies, employers are advised to adhere to the following principles of good practice and wherever appropriate, aim to incorporate them into a formal written agreement with trade union or employee representatives:

- *Give as much warning as possible.*
- *Consult with a recognised trade union, or with employee representatives in an attempt to avoid or minimise the need for redundancies.*
- *Where any reduction in labour is unavoidable, try to achieve it fairly and with as little hardship as possible.*
- *Look for alternatives to dismissal, such as the availability of other jobs, unless special circumstances render these measures impossible.*
- *Establish, in consultation with any union or employee representatives, the selection criteria and how such criteria will be applied.*
- *Ensure that the criteria are fair and objective and not dependent on the opinions of individuals.*

If you have been/or about to be made redundant you have certain legal entitlements.

The following is a summary of entitlements at the time of writing. **The information is offered in good faith and is believed to be accurate. No responsibility is accepted however, for the accuracy of the information, or the outcome of any consequential use of the information.**

Any employee with at least two years' continuous service of 16 hours or more per week (or five years' continuous service of eight hours or more per week) who is made redundant is entitled to:

- *redundancy pay*
- *appropriate notice*
- *time off to look for other work*
- *a trial period in any alternative job.*

Employers must notify independent trade unions of any forthcoming redundancies in writing.

Employers must pay at least the statutory minimum redundancy pay to employees so entitled.

The Employer must give a written statement to the employee showing how the redundancy payment has been calculated.

An employee is entitled to try any alternative job offered by the employer for a trial period of four weeks, which can be extended where necessary.

The means of selecting employees for redundancy must be fair, otherwise employees may be able to claim unfair redundancy.

To be fair, a redundancy must be:

- *genuine*
- *effected in accordance with company procedures*

- *following consultation with any trade union(s)*
- *subject to there being no alternative work available.*

Employers should give assistance with finding other work, either within the company or outside.

Offers of alternative employment need to take account of the employee's previous working conditions including pay, location, hours, status, etc.

The Department of Employment has published a series of booklets which cover various aspects of unemployment, e.g., a calculator for Statutory Redundancy Payments.

If you think that any aspect of your redundancy has been handled unfairly, I suggest that initially you take up your dissatisfaction with your previous employer.

If you are still unable to resolve your grievance, ACAS can advise you, free of charge. Contact their Head Office for the address and the telephone number of your regional office:

Advisory, Conciliation and Arbitration Service, 27 Wilton Street, London SW1X 7AZ. Tel: 071-210 3000 and ask for ACAS.

WOMEN RETURNERS

Citizens Advice Bureau – free advice about childcare, confidence-building, training.

The Career Changers Network of Women In Management. c/o Liz Harman, 64 Marryat Road, London SW19 5BN. Tel. 081-944 6332.

The Day-Care Trust/National Childcare Campaign. 4 Wild Court, London WC2B 5AU. Tel. 071-405 5617.

The National Extension College. 18 Brooklands Avenue, Cambridge CB2 2HN. Tel: 0223-316644. Open Learning Packages.

Working Mothers Association. 77 Holloway Road, London N7 8JZ. (Tel: 071-700 5771.) Returners' pack and information about childcare facilities.

Workplace Nurseries Ltd. 77 Holloway Road, London N7 8JZ. Tel: 071-700 0281. *Practical Guide to Workplace Nurseries*, price £10.00 inc. P&P, is available for purchase.

Your local College of Further Education – many run short courses to help with career and life planning and jobsearching.

WORKING FOR YOURSELF – ADVICE

Business in the Community. 227a City Road, London EC1V 1LX. Tel: 071 253 3716. In Scotland: **Scottish Business in the Community**, Romano House, 43 Station Road, Corstorphine, Edinburgh EH2 7AF. Tel 031-556 9761/2). Offers advice and information to people setting up a small business.

Fullemploy. County House, 190 Great Dover Street, London SE1 4YB. Tel: 071-378 1774. Telephone or write for details of your nearest training centre. A multi-ethnic organisation, it gives training and work experience in inner city area of England and Wales.

Instant Muscle. 84 Springside House, Northfield Road, London W14 9ES. Tel: 071 603 2604. A charity with offices in East Anglia, London, South Wales, Humberside, Yorkshire and the North West, which offers free business planning advice to unemployed 18-54 year olds.

Industrial Common Ownership Movement. Vassalli House, 20 Central Road, Leeds LS1 6DE. Tel: 0532 461738. Run by the National Federation of Workers Co-operatives, it provides information on how to start a co-operative.

Livewire. 60 Grainger Street, Newcastle Upon Tyne NE1 5JG. Tel: 091-261 5584. Offers free advice, planning action pack and personal adviser for 16-25 year olds, and annual cash awards of up to £3,000 for the best business plan.

Local Training & Enterprise Council and Local Enterprise Councils (TEC). (See telephone directory.) Offers advice in England, Wales and Scotland. For Northern Ireland contact the **Training and Employment Agency**, Clarendon House, 9-21 Adelaide Street, Belfast BT2 8DJ. Offers access to financial support, business training and consultancy.

Prince's Youth Business Trust. 5 The Pavement, Clapham, London SW4 0HY. Tel: 071-321 6500. In Scotland: **Prince's Scottish Youth Business Trust**, 6th Floor Mercantile Chambers, 53 Bothwell Street, Glasgow G2 6TS. Tel: 041-248 4999. Offers help for 18-25 year olds.

Rural Development Commission. See local telephone directory or contact: RDC, 141 Castle Street, Salisbury, Wilts SP1 3TP. Tel: 0722 336255. Offers help and advice for businesses setting up or operating outside main towns.

WORKING FOR YOURSELF – BOOKS

101 Ways to Suceed as an Independent Consultant, Timothy R.V. Foster, London Kogan Page.
Be Your Own Boss! David McMullan, London Kogan Page.
Buying a Company in Trouble, Ian Walker, Aldershot, Gower.
Croners Reference Book for the Self-employed, New Malden, Croner Publications Ltd.
Earning Money at Home, Edith Rudinger (ed.), London, the Consumers' Association.
Forming a Limited Company, Patricia Clayton, London, Kogan Page.
Franchising, R. Dixon, London, Pitman Publishing.
Getting Started, How to Set up your Own Business, Robson Rhodes, London, Kogan Page.
Going Freelance, Godfrey Golzen, London, Kogan Page.
Great Ideas for Making Money, Niki Chesworth, London, Kogan Page.
How to be a Consultant, Sally Garratt, Aldershot, Gower.
How to Set Up and Run your Own Business, Daily Telegraph, London, Kogan Page.
How to Make Money from Home, Peter Farrell, London, Kogan Page.
How to Make Money from Ideas and Inventions, R. Rogers, London, Kogan Page.
Letting Residential Property, Frances Way, London, Kogan Page.
Readymade Business Opportunities, Greg Clarke, London, Kogan Page.
Running a Home-Based Business, Dianne Baker, London, Kogan Page.
Running a Shop, Gary Jones, London, Pitman Publishing.
Small Business Survival, Roger Bennett, London, Pitman Publishing.
Start and Run a Profitable Consulting Business, Douglas A. Gray, London, Kogan Page.
Starting a Successful Small Business, M.J. Morris, London, Kogan Page.
Starting Up, Gary Jones, London, Pitman Publishing.
Survive and Prosper, Tony Boffey, London, Kogan Page.
Working for Yourself, Godfrey Golzen, London, Kogan Page.
Your Employment Rights, Michael Malone, London, Kogan Page.

WORKING FROM HOME

The National Homeworking Unit. Wolverley House, 18 Digbeth, Birmingham B5 6BJ. Tel: 021-643 6352. Advice on working from home.

SEMINARS AND CAREER COUNSELLING PROGRAMMES

Would you like to receive information on seminars and career counselling services based on *I Can Do That!*

These range from individual counselling, to workshops for groups, either for private individuals or as part of an organisation's redundancy programme.

For further information write to:
Malcolm Hornby c/o Pitman Professional Publishing,
128 Long Acre, London WC2E 9AN
Or fax your enquiry to 0327 858483

ORDER FORM: I CAN DO THAT!

		Price	Total
Please supply _____ copies of *I Can Do That!*		£14.95	
Postage and Packaging UK Addresses (Free on orders of 50 +)		£3.00	
Postage and Packaging Rest of World	Europe Air Mail Air Mail	£5.00/book £9.00/book	
TOTAL ORDER VALUE (including P&P)		£	

Deliver to:

Name _____

Address _____

_____ Postcode:_____ Telephone:_____

**TERMS: Payment with Order (cheque payable to Pitman Publishing)
or Charge to Visa or Mastercard**

Cardholder's Name _____ Card No. _____ Expiry Date _____

Cardholder's Signature _____

**Post your order to
Pitman Professional Publishing, 128 Long Acre, London WC2E 9AN, UK
Credit or Switch Card orders can be placed by fax or telephone:
Tel 071 379 7383   Fax 071 240 5771**